From
KITCHEN
to MARKET

From KITCHEN *to* MARKET

Selling Your Gourmet Food Specialty

STEPHEN F. HALL

Upstart Publishing Company, Inc.
The Small Business Publishing Company

Published by Upstart Publishing Company, Inc.
a division of Dearborn Publishing Group, Inc.
155 North Wacker Drive
Chicago, Illinois 60606-1719
(800)235-8866 or (312)836-4400

Library of Congress Cataloging-in-Publication Data

Hall, Stephen F.
      From kitchen to market: selling your gourmet food specialty /
Stephen F. Hall.
            p.   cm.
      Includes index
      ISBN: 0-936894-34-2 : $24.95
            1. Food industry and trade -- United States. 2. Food service -
- United States.   I. Title
HD9004.H25 1992
664'.0068'8--dc20   92-29069
                                                     CIP

Printed in the United States of America
10 9 8 7 6 5 4

Book design by Brad Robeson

For a complete catalog of Upstart's small business publications call, (800) 235-8866.

First and foremost, I am grateful to my wife, Patricia Teagle, for her unending good humor and editorial counsel. Many thanks, also, to my colleagues in the specialty food business, particularly Ron Johnson, of Gourmet America, Inc., who provided important viewpoints in defining how specialty food marketing works; Elliot Johnson, of Mark T. Wendell Co., for the precision with which he assesses industry trends; Liz and Nick Thomas, of Chalif, Inc., who provided comprehensive and altogether helpful reviews of the first draft of this guide; Barry Raskin, a specialty food broker largely responsible for guiding me during my early education in this field; Ernie Fisher, an international food consultant who brought a "real world" perspective to examining this industry; and to Lee Robinson, who, as President of The Ruffled Truffle, provided me with the opportunity to learn about the gift segment of the specialty food business.

I am grateful, further, to Page Pratt, co-founder of Food Marketing International, with whom I shared many a rewarding marketing moment, and to my editor, Jean Kerr, whose unflappable disposition eased the burden of perfecting this book.

Finally, I would like to acknowledge my late colleague, classmate and best friend, Rolff Johansen, for bringing civility and wit to our hectic earlier years in specialty food marketing.

TABLE OF CONTENTS

Appendices

HOW TO USE THIS GUIDE

From Kitchen To Market helps you learn about marketing food, a process that generally entails everything from product concept to after-sales service.

In addition to packaging, labeling, pricing, storage and shipping, the guide tells you how to advertise, promote and sell your product. Flow charts describe how to process the orders you generate. Major sections include "Guidelines for Success" that you may use as you prepare to take your product to market.

From Kitchen to Market is designed principally for small, cottage industries new to the food business, but it will also be of significant value to large food processors and overseas food companies interested in learning how the U.S. specialty food trade functions.

Specialty food marketing is addressed in a straightforward, logical manner. It begins with introductory comments, followed by a general discussion of the industry. It proceeds to discuss the issues relevant to getting your product ready to market, and to taking your product to market. The appendices offer information about additional sources of assistance along with useful data regarding trade shows, trade journals, co-packers, etc.

Other helpful resources from Upstart Publishing include *The Business Planning Guide: Creating a Plan for Success in Your Own Business. The Business Planning Guide* leads business owners through the most important step in founding a new business: putting together a complete and effective business plan and financing proposal.

Also, *The Start Up Guide: A One-Year Plan for Entrepreneurs,* provides a practical timetable for covering all the basics before opening a new business. And, *On Your Own: A Woman's Guide to Building a Business,* is for women who want hands-on, practical information about starting and running a business. It deals honestly with issues such as finding time for your business when you are the primary care provider, societal biases against women, and credit discrimination. All of these books are especially useful in planning and running any small business.

You will probably not need this guide if your name is Paul Newman. Deep pockets can make the difference between success or failure for a high quality product. If, like the rest of us, you have neither the funding level to support a major marketing effort, nor the clout to see it through, then this guide is for you.

Before you begin—Do you want your food operation to be a full time occupation or a sideline business?

One of the following scenarios may describe your circumstances, and could help you respond to the important issue of just how involved you would like to become in the business. All four of these scenarios have been played out, with varying degrees of success, in the gourmet food industry.

❖ **Scenario One**: You have just returned from another successful holiday church bazaar where you sold out your homemade supply of apple-cranberry chutney. Your chutney is based on a family recipe handed down for generations. Your friends and neighbors urge you to sell your chutney to Bloomingdale's, where they think it will be a great hit. You think it's a wonderful idea, but you haven't the foggiest idea of where to begin.

In this scenario, the entrepreneur has to decide, after significant investigation, whether or not to continue in the "sideline" mode, or to take the risk of turning the operation into a full-time business.

On the one hand, the owner has a product that has been tested, in a fashion, with positive reactions from customers, friends, and neighbors. There is reason to believe that success, at least initially, might be achieved with a reasonable expectation of profit. On the other hand, what is the required level of funding available for the venture? If the owner has an outside source of income, then the venture may be undertaken. Otherwise, the possibilities for negative cash flow (more money going out than coming in) are quite probable.

❖ **Scenario Two**: Your gourmet food store is doing a lot of business. You are especially pleased with the success of your prepared foods section, one item of which is your home-baked, seasoned, bread sticks. You note that there seems to be a growing interest in this product from a broad segment of your customer base. You wonder if it would be possible to sell the bread sticks to a wider audience in other markets in your region. Where to begin?

If the second scenario fits, then your food marketing venture could be supported by revenues from the existing retail operation. This makes market entry more attractive because many initial costs of operation could be absorbed by the retail store sales of other products. Nevertheless, you will have to devote substantial time to developing markets for the bread sticks, which will take away from time spent in the store. If this can be accommodated, then a full-time sales and marketing operation can be adopted.

❖ **Scenario Three**: You have recently taken over a small, local, chocolate manufacturer. Until now, revenues have come from bulk sales to walk-in and mail-order customers. You think there are substantial opportunities for developing a retail packaged version, and you want to begin distributing it to stores all over the country. How do you proceed?

Scenario three offers some of the same challenges as scenario two. Both require substantial time at the existing business. Scenario three, however, offers a chance to expand an existing base of sales to customers located outside of the local area. It also provides an existing source of revenue (from retail-packaged sales) on which to base some of the expansion costs. It would appear, then, that turning the chocolate operation into a full-time sales and marketing operation might be an appropriate alternative.

❖ **Scenario Four**: Your family and friends love your honey and pecan mustard. You have been very successful in selling at the local Women's Exchange, and at area school holiday fairs. You also ran an ad in a slick "upscale" magazine that cost you a fortune, but produced results in mail-order sales sufficient to cover the cost. Your life is too busy to contemplate going into the gourmet food business full time. What do you need to know about this business in order to make a little money on the side?

The challenge in Scenario Four is to make your hobby into a sideline business. You can take your talent, your recipes, your promotional genius, and your money, and have your product produced, packaged, warehoused, and marketed by another company. You will definitely need the supporting funds and the knowledge of how gourmet food marketing works.

Your situation may differ from these scenarios, but the opportunity to turn your food ideas into an endeavor for financial independence prevails. The gourmet food business is one way of obtaining a significant shot at achieving success and acquiring wealth.

Now that you are armed with a sense of which option best applies to your situation, read on to learn how to take the next step in the exciting and challenging world of gourmet food marketing.

A Note about the Illustrations

Product appearance is one of the most important components of success in the specialty food industry. In order to give you a flavor of this, and to stimulate your imagination, I have included a representative sampling of graphics used in a variety of specialty food labels, packages, and company logos. These have been placed throughout the book, in no particular order.

The illustrations selected were among those requested from seventy-five companies whose products appeared in the National Association for the Specialty Food Trade *What's New? 1992* publication.

A number of these are designed for application in color, but, because of cost constraints, they have been reproduced here in black and white. Many of them are effective attention-getters with the use of only two colors. The objective is to emphasize the importance of graphics, regardless of color, in label, package, and logo design.

The examples in this book are those deemed typical, both good and, perhaps, not so good, for this industry. You be the judge. And, please note that use of them does not constitute an endorsement.

From
KITCHEN
to MARKET

INTRODUCTION

The specialty foods industry is generating retail revenues of almost $10 billion a year. To some, this means great opportunity. To others, it represents a formidable challenge.

Your ability to grab a slice of this pie, and make your mark, establish your independence, achieve success, and acquire wealth will depend on how effectively you prepare—and prepare you must!

How to prepare for the opportunities and challenges of taking your food products to the appropriate store shelves is the subject of this guide. You need not know the basics of small business operations just yet. For now, success will depend on your drive, talent, and the amount of capital you can raise.

Let's put this into perspective: The average cost of getting national grocery store shelf exposure for a new product by a branded manufacturer is $5.1 million, as stated in a recent study by a Joint Industry Task Force consisting of the Grocery Manufacturers of America, Food Marketing

Institute, National American Wholesale Grocers Association, National Association of Chain Drug Stores, National Food Brokers Association, and National Grocer Association.

Still reading? Take heart, there is a proven alternative. It is the specialty food industry that has become the vehicle for entry level food distribution in the United States. Different market segments and new products can be tested in this industry without the initial investment required of the major food producers.

How much will it cost you? Depending on your approach, you can expect to incur minimum start-up costs of approximately $25,000 to $100,000 each year for the first three to five years. This includes production, packaging, labeling, advertising and promotion of one product. The estimated cost is based on the assumption that you will be doing *a lot* of the leg work. (Example: You do all of the administrative, invoicing, clerical paperwork, etc., and you make most of the sales calls.)

"You'll need more than a dream to carry you across the starting line."
—Liz Thomas, Former Exec. VP, Chalif, Inc.

"You'll need more than a dream to carry you across the starting line," says Liz Thomas, Former Exec. VP, Chalif, Inc.

Our purpose is to explore the inner workings of "niche" marketing. Niche marketing entails finding the best combination of product packaging, pricing, positioning and promotion that will encourage the consumer to purchase a product not otherwise offered by the major suppliers. Imagination is a key ingredient, but adequate funding is essential.

In addition to the above, a successful undertaking requires you to center your activities on your competitive strengths, control your costs, know your competition, and learn how to manage the entire process effectively.

We are not addressing here what you can do with a several million dollar budget. Rather, this guide deals with the essence of entrepreneurship.

There is a lot of "ready, fire, aim" in the gourmet food marketing process that can lead to some success and frequent failure. This guide helps you accomplish most of the "aiming" during the "ready" phase.

Specialty food marketing requires creative responses. As soon as you adopt a successful marketing strategy, you may learn of another entrepreneur who is just as successful, but who has implemented an entirely different marketing scheme!

"The Specialty Food business is an odd little segment of the industry that is better left to people who understand it fully, who deeply care about it, and who are willing to have a less predictable bottom line than most corporations are willing to tolerate," says Ted Koryn, specialty food marketing professional as quoted in *Fortune* magazine, October 1978.

CHAPTER ONE
INDUSTRY BACKGROUND

This chapter examines and identifies the primary sales territories and segments of the market. A description of transition products—those that make the transition from gourmet to grocery (the "big time")—is included, along with a discussion of a typical gourmet retail store operation.

DEFINITIONS

The food industry, in general, and the specialty food industry, in particular, have yet to sanction specific guidelines for the use of many industry terms. As a result, the process of tracking and understanding the myriad elements of specialty food sales and marketing activity has yielded additional challenges to those trying to understand the industry.

Gourmet: This guide uses the term "gourmet" sparingly, and as a synonym for "specialty."

Specialty Food: The National Association for the Specialty Food Trade has adopted the following description of specialty foods:

Specialty food products . . . shall mean: foods, beverages or confections meant for human use that are of the highest grade, style and/or quality in their category. Their specialty nature derives from a combination of some or all of the following qualities: their uniqueness, exotic origin, particular processing, design, limited supply, unusual application or use, extraordinary packaging or channel of distribution . . . , the common denominator of which is their unusually high quality.

Specialty food is the traditionally accepted term meaning food products that fit the following criteria:

High quality: Above all, the specialty food product must be of the highest quality, in both content and form. As a rule, only the best ingredients are used, whether the product is a premium ice cream or a mustard with peppercorns. Specialty food products sold at retail must also look the part—a high price demands that the product appear to be fancy and high tone.

High price: Most specialty foods are priced higher than staple food products because of costly ingredients and labor used in their preparation. Others are high in cost because of high demand and limited supply. Still others are sold at high prices because of the low turnover they generate in retail stores (the longer they remain on the shelf, the more they cost the retailer).

Limited availability: Many specialty foods have appeal because they are not generally available. Such foods often gain a cult status—fresh caviar is an example—in that they offer the consumer a cachet not offered by products sold everywhere.

Imported or unique: Imported specialty foods maintain a strong hold on the market, even though the trend appears headed away from imported products. Many high quality products are now produced in this country and retain the "imported" distinction that first brought them to U.S. consumers' attention.

Food Producer/Processor: The producer is usually the grower, and the processor is the one who adds value by processing the raw commodity into a table-ready food product.

Food Broker: A commissioned sales representative, usually with broad experience in the food industry, who generally calls mostly on distributors and large retail chains.

Specialty Food Distributor: A company that buys in volume, for its own account, and sells to retailers (and to other distributors).

Store-Door Delivery: Delivery made to stores by distributors.

Direct Store Distributor: A distributor who performs many of the same services as a jobber (described in this section).

Wholesaler: Companies that contract with, for example, a chain supermarket to warehouse and deliver a product that has been sold by the food producer to the supermarket. Wholesalers usually buy the product only when the producer has sold it to the supermarket chain. It is highly unlikely that you will have to deal with wholesalers because most of them are not equipped to handle the very detailed nature of specialty food merchandising.

Rack Jobbers: These are the people you see in supermarkets stocking shelves (they are the ones with the suits and ties, as opposed to supermarket employees). They price the incoming merchandise with price stickers (in those states where this is still required), fix shelf labels, follow schematic diagrams approved by the store, remove damaged and returned merchandise, and stock and dust the shelves.

Customers: Retailers and Distributors.

Consumers: "Our reason for existing."

PRIMARY MARKETS

Sales of specialty foods tend to be concentrated in the more affluent market areas, because of the relatively high retail prices involved. The available market research identifies forty primary trade areas of this type, and the majority of your prospective clients will fall within them.

A variety of different retail outlets have the potential to handle specialty food products. So called "gourmet shops" are the most obvious, but there are also cheese shops, delicatessens, gift stores and, in increasing numbers, supermarkets and department stores.

Supermarkets in the Midwest have tended to play a stronger role in the specialty food trade than have supermarkets in other parts of the country. Their imported, ethnic, or specialty foods sections are often quite large and offer a diversified selection of items. As a corollary, gourmet shops are fewer in that region.

Recently, however, many more supermarkets in all major trading areas have taken on so-called gourmet products. Over the past five years, some of the nation's largest supermarket chains, such as Safeway, Kroger, Vons, and Giant Foods have invested significantly in expanding their shelf space to carry specialty foods. Safeway, Vons, and Giant have opened separate specialty food stores. Safeway's are called Bon Appetit, Giant's are called Someplace Special, and Von's are called Von's Pavilions. Each offers a mix of high quality staples, "picture perfect" fresh produce, frozen foods and specialty items. The industry is watching these ventures with an eye to adopting new directions in distributing specialty foods.

There are approximately 150,000 food stores in the United States, and only 23,000 of them can be considered prime prospects for specialty food products. This figure results from careful, conservative paring down of the raw data presented in business directories. The total of prime prospects is composed of approximately 4,800 gourmet shops, 7,300 cheese shops and health food stores, 7,500 delicatessens, and 3,400 chain supermarket outlets, gift shops and major department stores.

Case In Point

Blanchard & Blanchard - Vermont-based line of salad dressings, dessert sauce, mustard, marinades, ketchup and cocktail sauces. Full line with attractive, upscale, packaging. Significant promotion dollars invested. Attempted wide distribution with some success in grocery market. Refined line in 1990. Now focused on specialty food distribution.

Primary Trade Areas (in order of primacy)

(Copyright *The New Yorker* magazine, Inc.)

New York	San Diego	Hartford
Los Angeles	Denver	New Orleans
Chicago	Baltimore	Sacramento
San Francisco	Atlanta	Columbus
Detroit	Pittsburgh	Indianapolis
Washington	St. Louis	Oklahoma City
Philadelphia	Phoenix	San Antonio
Houston	Milwaukee	Salt Lake City
Boston	Portland	Charlotte
Miami/Fort Lauderdale	Kansas City	Allentown/Bethlehem
Dallas/Fort Worth	Riverside/San Bernadino	Buffalo
Seattle-Tacoma	Cincinnati	West Palm Beach
Cleveland-Akron	Honolulu	
Minneapolis-St. Paul	Tampa/St. Petersburg	

Primary U.S. Specialty Food Markets

This map of primary U.S. specialty food markets provides a visual representation that will assist you in directing your marketing efforts. Note that several entire states can be virtually ignored during your initial introductory efforts.

It would be unlikely for you to reach all of these prime prospects without national distribution capability, either on your own, or through a major specialty food distributor.

In view of the "upscale" nature of specialty food product lines, primary marketing targets can be identified by using weighted rankings of *The New Yorker* magazine Selected Marketing System. This identifies and ranks markets for quality, premium-priced products, rather than simply ranking markets by total population and income data.

The forty primary trade areas listed in this chapter are the most important United States markets for quality merchandise. About 15,000 of the 23,000 prime prospects are located in these areas. The listing is an accurate reflection of the trade in general.

Although a strictly specialty food ranking would include all of those listed, the order in which they are listed would be somewhat different.

MARKET SEGMENTS

Our identification of geographic/demographic markets for specialty food represents one of the first elements of the marketing process. These markets are further segmented by matters of consumer preference, ethnic division, population movement, taste and historical trends.

To illustrate, hot and spicy foods have long been accepted in the Southwest; whereas, they are gaining a strong foothold in New England markets. In Southern California, everybody eats outdoors where the barbecue and barbecue products reign! And it is difficult to introduce a new product to Floridians in the summer when specialty food business tends to fall off drastically.

HEALTH FOOD STORES: The mounting importance of health food stores should be taken into account. Distribution channels for health foods differ in some cases. Some distributors carry only health food lines, while others only service the more upscale channels of distribution; e.g., fancy gourmet food stores. There are profitable opportunities to be explored in this segment of the industry if your product meets its criteria.

THE GIFT TRADE: The gift trade is also playing a greater part in specialty food marketing. Available data indicate more than 70,000 gift or gift-type stores in the entire country. This figure includes both upscale and standard outlets. As with health food stores, distribution channels can differ in that segment.

Much of the gift trade is served by the food rep (broker) who maintains a showroom, attends and exhibits at gift shows, and calls extensively on retail accounts. Such brokers are paid a 15% commission of the invoice value of all sales to retailers made in accordance with the broker contract.

An overall understanding of these differing market segments and varying distribution requirements will be helpful to you as you plan your marketing and distribution strategy.

ETHNIC FOODS: For our purposes, Ethnic Foods means retail and food service packaged food products that can be described generally as either Italian, Hispanic, Kosher, Oriental, or Greek.

Italian-style foods comprise one of the largest categories, and Italian ingredients have become one of the basics of our everyday cuisine. Because of this, there is an enormous market for Italian foods. But, is there room for another pasta or olive oil?

The United States is said to be the fifth largest Spanish-speaking country in the world. Our Hispanic population exceeds twenty-four million and is the fastest growing consumer market. The best products for growth will be staples advertised and promoted in Spanish by the major food producer/processors. Your opportunity will lie in the growing interest in Hispanic and Hispanic-style foods and cooking.

The Kosher food market exceeded $2 billion in 1992, and it is expected to continue its ten percent plus annual growth. The broad appeal of Kosher foods beyond that which is mandated by Jewish dietary practice is based on the quality associated with such foods. In order to be certified Kosher, a food product must pass an exacting inspection by an authorized Rabbinical agency.

American consumer interest in health and fitness has spurred growth of foods that are unprocessed and fresh. This includes a great number of oriental foods. The market for this category exceeds $1 billion at retail. Among the leading oriental food

Case In Point

Freixenet Sparkling Wine from Spain—Introduced by Specialty Foods and Beverages Company. Solidly distributed in the specialty food trade. Hit the market at a time when consumers were looking for an attractively packaged, good tasting, low-priced "champagne." Now available throughout the country. This is a transition product.

products are vegetables, sauces, and dry mixes. Increasing home use of stir-fry is also encouraging oriental food consumption. Today, once exotic foods such as ginger root, oriental vegetables, tempura sauce, and bean sprouts are readily available.

Greek foods, also referred to as "Mediterranean" cuisine, are growing in popularity because of their traditional reliance on freshness. Some examples include olive oil, cheese, honey, dressings, and baked goods.

Your opportunity with the ethnic food category may be twofold: (1) produce and market traditional ethnic food products not otherwise available to consumers, and/or (2) market new "ethnic-style" products to both ethnic and "non-ethnic" consumers.

TRANSITION PRODUCTS

Many specialty food producers are attracted to the idea that their product will capture public imagination and sell like crazy. They envision the day when everyone will beat a path to their door demanding their product! When, and if, this happens (and it can happen), the product will reach a transition stage from up-market specialty food distribution to down-market grocery trade.

In some markets, your product will continue to be merchandised as a specialty item, while in others, it will be sold solely on grocery/supermarket shelves.

Recent examples of transition products include Perrier Water, Grey Poupon Mustard, Red Oval Stoned Wheat Thins, Cadbury Chocolate Bars, and Häagen-Dazs Ice Cream.

GOURMET STORE CONCERNS

Your understanding of how your product is merchandised (placed before the consumer in the retail

Case In Point

Mr. and Mrs. "T" Bloody Mary Mix—Introduced by Taylor Foods. A big hit. Now the brand is owned by Heublein and marketed everywhere. This is a successful example of a "transition" product.

store) will influence the direction of all your marketing efforts. Having some knowledge of how a typical retail gourmet food store operates will enable you to work more effectively with your distributors, brokers, and with the store manager.

Product selection will depend on store type and on a variety of demographic conditions. Certain food products are in higher demand in certain regions. If you are selling your version of a hot salsa, then you will probably have better luck by introducing it to New England fancy food stores than to those in the Southwest, where a "million" such products are well established in grocery distribution.

Specialty Food Store Classifications

Type	Classification
Upscale Deli	Delicatessen foods and associated condiments.
Specialty	Gourmet foods, sometimes with specific upscale product lines (coffee, for example).
Cheese	All kinds of cheese and related items.
Gift	Gift baskets.
Housewares	Gourmet pots and pans and other cookware, with some impulse and companion food items.
Department	Upscale with heavy emphasis on cookware and some confectionery. (Demonstrations play a key role in cookware sales.)
General	Combination of all of the above, including some traditional staples.

The average gourmet store generally sells a mix of products along the following lines:

Product Line	Approximate Percentage of Sales
Condiments	40%
Beverages (including bottled water)	5%
Coffee and tea	5%
Cheese	5%
Pâtés and meats	10%
Prepared foods	15%
Confection	10%
Other	10%
	100%

As a rule, the manager of a small specialty food store will work very long hours, in effect "marrying" the store. Many of the most successful retail specialty food enterprises are operated by families—for obvious reasons. You may be interested in knowing how the "average" manager spends her/his time:

8A.M. to Noon	Ordering/opening/training Food preparation
Noon to 2P.M.	Luncheon sales
2P.M. to 7P.M.	General administration/baking supplier meetings (this is you)

Your role is to operate for the convenience of the retailer, who, in turn, operates for the convenience of the consumer.

Supplier's Role

The Boston Restaurant Group* suggests the following guidelines for you to follow:

❖ *Become Involved.*
Get to know the particular challenges confronting each key retailer.

❖ *Educate the Buyer.*
Provide point-of-purchase materials. Arrange to spend some time with the sales staff.

❖ *Follow-up on Deliveries.*
Determine if all went well.

❖ *Follow-up on Shortages.*
Ascertain if still needed and fill orders.

❖ *Develop Seasonal Guidelines.*
Find out what works best, where.

❖ *Agree to Minimum Orders.*
Be prepared to "break" cases.

❖ *Try to Allow Exclusivity.*
Try not to sell same product to competitor across the street.

Average opening costs for a 1,000 square-foot store:

Leasehold, Improvements	$45,000
Equipment	30,000
Start-up	10,000
Inventory	15,000
Total	$100,000

*A company involved in the purchase, sale, and management of restaurants and retail gourmet food stores.

CHAPTER TWO
GETTING READY TO MARKET

This chapter considers start-up costs, consumer demand, and the market research required before you undertake a large production run for your product. The chapter also examines product categories in demand, and it addresses the issues of producing, packaging, labeling, and pricing your product. A description of warehousing, inventory, and shipping is also included.

START-UP COSTS

Here's an important piece of advice that is based on fifteen years of gourmet food sales and marketing experience: You must have an independent source of income to successfully start your own gourmet food marketing business! You should have sufficient capital available to cover all your costs for the first three to five years. This includes all normal living expenses.

Your start-up costs will depend on your circumstances and on the type of product you plan to market.

And even in light of such information, your specific start-up costs will be difficult to peg. As you will see in the following pages, our estimate ranges from $25,000 to $100,000 per year for the first three years.

If you will be using your own kitchen facility, you can save money until your production requirements outstrip your kitchen's capability. After that, you will want to negotiate with a food packer/processor to have your product produced to meet the increased demand. The same goes for other overhead and administrative costs. You should take advantage of existing office space and equipment, and you might be able to use friends to help out part-time.

The people referred to in Scenarios Two and Three, at the beginning of this book, had offices, production facilities, and administrative capability. They were also operating an existing business.

Start-up costs encompass production, packaging, warehousing, administration, and product advertising and promotion costs. The specific cost categories include those listed in the accompanying "Guidelines for Success."

The data in the table on this page gives you an idea of cost elements used by the major leaguers. They cover costs of obtaining nationwide grocery distribution of warehouse-sourced products, and they do not include costs of direct-store delivered items. Your cost percentages will be lower in advertising and consumer promotion, while higher by about fifteen percent in the trade deals and allowances segment. In the end, trade advertising, promotion, and deals will constitute the major portion of your costs.

Cost Elements of New Product Introduction by a *Major Producer*

Element	% of Costs
Advertising and Consumer Promotion	46%
Trade Deals and Allowances	16%
Market Research and Product Development	18%
Other	20%
	100%

Source: "Managing the Process of Introducing and Deleting Products in the Grocery and Drug Industry," Joint Industry Task Force, 1990. Grocery Manufacturers of America, Inc.

GUIDELINES FOR SUCCESS
Start-Up Cost Analysis
Use these guidelines to determine your start-up costs.

Item	Cost Saving Considerations	Monthly Cost Estimate
Postage	Almost all of your mail will be first class. If you plan to do a lot of mail-order selling, then ask the post office for information about postage-paid and bulk mail privileges.	$50.00
Travel	You can reduce your travel costs by carefully planning your itinerary. Expect to make no more than four sales calls per day. Use a telephone whenever possible.	400.00
Office supplies	You will need a word processor, desk, chair, telephone, laser printer, forms, bond paper, pens/pencils, files, etc.	200.00
Promotion material	Catalog sheets, price lists, neck tags (possibly). Prepare your own press releases. Do not advertise to the consumer unless you do mail order. Restrict trade ads to a complete—well-managed—promo campaign. Otherwise save your money to make sales calls.	125.00
Telephone	If you do any trade advertising, for example, the phone company will require you to install a business line. Ask for information on an "800" number, but do not install one until you are certain that it will be used a lot.	150.00
Fax	Many local office supply stores can provide you with fax service for a per sheet price. Or, consider using a friend's fax.	50.00
Utilities	Pro-rate your current utility cost to cover that used by the business (if office in home).	100.00

Item	Cost Saving Considerations	Monthly Cost Estimate
Rent	If your office is to be in your home, take a percentage of your monthly mortgage equal to the space occupied by your office. That will be your monthly rent.	600.00
Product ingredients	Try to arrange minimum bulk shipments. Ask your supplier to store the ingredients and to invoice you only when you draw down the supply.	Product Dependent
Product packaging	Find other companies that are producing a product in a container similar to yours. Try to realize economies of scale by ordering a large quantity and splitting the shipment between, or among, the other companies.	Product Dependent
Labels	Labeling by hand during your initial stage will save you money. It will also allow you to experiment with different labels without having to order 10,000 of one kind, only to find out they won't work. You will require the talents of a good graphic artist.	Product Dependent
Miscellaneous	All the rest. Figure about 10% of total costs.........................	Product Dependent

Notes to start-up cost analysis

These costs do not include cost of labor, most of which will be borne by you. Other costs of production, including inventory management, site selection, and quality control should be considered if you will be establishing your own production facility. Also, the rent figure ($600.00 per month) can be deferred, since it will be you paying yourself. The same goes for utilities.

The office supplies include initial purchase of a computer, word processing and related software, telephone answering machine, printer, adding machine, etc. The conservative, annualized, figure is $2400. You may be able to do better with used or something other than top-of-the-line equipment.

The grand total, not including production (ingredients, packaging, labeling, labor) or miscellaneous, comes to just over $17,000. This allows approximately $8,000 to $83,000 to cover the production element, bringing the estimated total to between $25,000 and $100,000 for each of the first three year dollar requirements.

Producers Respond: How Long Does it Take and How Much Does it Cost?

Chautauqua Hills Jelly Company *packs and distributes jams, jellies, chocolate sauces. The company started with $100,000, but would have preferred $150,000. It recommends $100,000 to $150,000 per year for 3 to 5 years for success, and submits the following as a successful specialty food product line: Pasta Mamma's gourmet pasta and sauces.*

International Marketing Services *is an importer and distributor of a broad line of specialty foods, and is the master distributor of Blanchard & Blanchard products. It came under new management and ownership about three years ago. The company suggests three years for success, with $50,000 to $60,000 required per year.*

The Herb Patch Ltd. *has spent the past eleven years producing instant cocoa mixes, flavored honeys, salt free culinary blends, herbal teas and vinegars. It names the following as examples of successful specialty food products: Honey Acres (honey and honey mustard), D.L. Jardines (full line of Texas foods), and Maple Grove (pure maple syrup and maple syrup products).*

Pelican Bay Ltd. *says it could not afford to do it if it started today. The company produces and markets unique blends of all natural herbs and spices for dips, seasonings, drink mixes, and mixes for children. Advises that it would take upwards of five years for a new entrant to succeed.*

Peachtree Specialty Foods *has produced an extensive line of condiments and sauces for the past three years. Company reports that it is still struggling to get into the black. Very high quality ingredients and packaging. Exhibits in many trade shows. Recommends newcomer stake of $25,000 to $30,000 per year get into this industry.*

Pasta Mamma's *derives some of its revenue base from a 2,500 square foot retail food business. It produces and sells fresh, dried, flavored gourmet pasta and sauces. It has been in business four years, and reports that it can take three to five years before success can be attained. "The amount of money required depends on the attitude and focus of the owner/manager who must be willing to listen, follow-up, and make cold sales calls."*

John Wm. Macy's Cheesesticks *produces hand-rolled sourdough cheesesticks. In business seven years, and in the black for the past three years. Recommends beginning firms invest approximately $50,000 per year for first three to four years.*

Goldwater's Foods of Arizona, Inc. *markets Goldwater's "Taste of the Southwest," Sedona Red Salsas, Paradise Pineapple Salsa, and Rio Verde Tomatillo Salsa. It recommends beginners invest $250,000 over a seven year period to succeed. Proposes the following as a successful specialty food product line: Peggy-Jane's Salad Dressing (now marketed by Knotts Berry Farm).*

Grace Tea Company, Ltd. *distributes Grace Rare Teas. The company principal says: "About money, it is best to try to use someone else's." He advises entrants to* *raise $100,000 to $150,000 per year for the first six years to succeed.*

Golden Walnut Specialty Food *has been marketing specialty foods for five years. It sells Golden Walnut cookies, shortbread Almond Ingot cakes, and cheesecakes. Reports that it is now operating in the black. The company principal comments that he was "very surprised at how complex and competitive" is the specialty food market.*

Harney & Sons, Ltd. *distributes Connoisseur fine teas. This company is a focused, niche player. It began by selling only to institutional accounts (mostly hotels and private clubs) through personal networking. The owner points out that the amount of money to succeed depends on too many variables to pin down, and suggests that success for a beginner will take at least three years.*

Ridley's Muffin Chips *produced its initial revenues from a retail muffin store. Demand for their leftover muffin pieces grew so fast that product was reformulated into a muffin chip. This one is a success. They made a product hit from a mistake.*

RESEARCHING THE MARKET— IDENTIFYING CONSUMER DEMAND

One of your first and most important forays into the marketplace will be to determine the strength of demand for your product. You will also want to see who else is marketing a similar product (the competition), and at what price, in what packaging, and with what sort of promotional support.

Weigh the following market research considerations, and keep your findings in mind as you make your production, packaging, labeling, pricing, and inventory and shipping arrangements. Explore the issues of how the industry works, and acquire information that will provide you with a solid foundation about:

- ◆ major participants,
- ◆ recent trends,
- ◆ prospects for a product such as yours,
- ◆ technical and production requirements,
- ◆ regulatory influence (food and drug laws),
- ◆ competitive situation, and
- ◆ industry advertising and promotion methods.

Be prepared to gather as much information and data as possible about the potential for your product. Do not underestimate the value of networking. A lot of specialty food producers and marketers will be happy to share their experiences and insights with you.

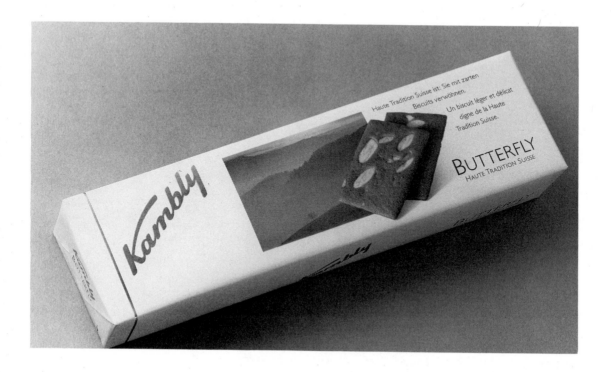

GUIDELINES FOR SUCCESS
Market Research

Objective	Resources/Procedures
Define and analyze the specialty foods industry.	Visit major specialty food industry trade shows, especially those sponsored by the National Association for the Specialty Food Trade (NASFT).
Identify industry participants: producers, distributors, brokers, retailers, and consumers.	Visit shows and review this guide. Gather information from the NASFT.
Develop overview of major trends. Understand current changes in consumer requirements for specialty foods, in general, and for the food category you have in mind, in particular.	Review industry trade journals (see Appendix B of this guide).
Describe important suppliers especially those with whom you will be competing. Understand the various sales, marketing, and distribution strategies they employ.	Visit food shows. Ask questions. Take notes.
Review impact of technology on the entire marketing process, including production, packaging, and order processing. What are the technological implications for your application?	For example, will your ingredients require special machinery to process? Will the package you have selected require special orders from high-tech packaging companies? Contact the Institute of Food Technologies, 221 N. Lasalle St., Chicago, IL 60601 (312-782-8424).

Objective	Resources/Procedures
Describe regulatory influence on the production, packaging, labeling, and marketing of your intended product.	Check your state's regulation & FDA for sanitary certification. Check Chapter 21 of Federal Code of Regulations (CFR) for labeling and ingredient statements. Most states prohibit the use of your own kitchen. A separate facility is required.

Upscale Products with the Greatest Growth Potential

Appetizers/hors d'oeuvres
Candy
Cereals
Coffee
Chocolate
Crackers/cookies
Beverages
Value added meat/poultry
Bottled water
Fruit
Exotic mushrooms
Ice cream/sorbet
Non-alcoholic beverages
Nuts
Pasta
Oils/vinegars
Seafood
Salsa/hot sauces
Pâté
Beverages (concentrates)
Salad dressings
Sauces/bases
Juices
Seasonings/spices/herbs
Tea
Breads
Cakes/pastry
Vegetables

DEVELOPING THE PRODUCT

Marketing strategies will differ depending on whether your product is fresh, refrigerated or frozen. Also, matters of "shelf life"—the time it takes for your product to deteriorate—will have to be considered. For example, chocolate products are traditionally sold and shipped during cooler seasons. Otherwise, the cost of shipping can escalate and place your chocolate product out of the competition. A product with a short shelf life will have to move off the shelf faster. To insure this may require a considerable promotional expenditure.

A comprehensive market profile appears in Appendix Q. The profile discusses major specialty food product categories in terms of configuration, types, recent trends, size, market share, and other considerations. You will find it useful to review the category in which you hold an interest in order to become better informed about your prospects for success.

On the left is a listing of upscale products rated with the highest growth potential. Those products with the greatest growth potential tend to be high quality, convenient foods. They are foods that are perceived, for the most part, as being healthy, or healthier than others, while offering the benefit of a special "treat."

Product Positioning

The term "product positioning" covers the overall concept of how your product will be marketed. It includes the pricing, packaging, labeling, and advertising and promotion considerations. For example, a Cajun-style food might better be positioned as a gift/souvenir, when sold in New Orleans, than merely as a food product. It would be positioned in such a way as to attract attention of tourists. Successful positioning has to do with your best assessment of what benefit you will be providing to your prospective consumer. How to appeal to this consumer is the point of product positioning.

There are many examples. Who knew that bottled water would make such headway in the United States? Our tap water is supposed to be perfectly safe and wholly acceptable for all of our water needs. Then, in the 1970's, Source Perrier invested an estimated $3 million to position its bottled water as an alternative to tap water, and, even more importantly, as an alternative to alcohol in bars and restaurants. Perrier is bottled in a unique container, imported from France, and it commands a higher price than its competition. Yet it has developed a commanding lead in its market . . . all by effective product positioning.

The point of positioning is to differentiate your product. Everyone knows about the apple. Yes, it is healthy. Yes, it is inexpensive. Yes, it is available at every grocery in the nation. So, if you have a new "apple," then you will have to differentiate it from the others. Doing this is called product positioning. Think hard about novel means of packaging and promoting it. Remember the "Pet Rock"? Read "Pliskin's Phables" for an effective and amusing description of product positioning.

Upscale Products with the Least Growth Potential

Alcoholic beverages
Condiments (except certain sauces and salsas)
Dessert toppings
Jams / jellies and preserves
Rice
Soups
Syrups / honey

Pliskin's Phables:
How Positioning Began

(With thanks to Mr. Pliskin)

Case In Point

The Infamous Cookie was exhibited by Duchess Farms Company at the 1977 National Fancy Food and Confection Show in New Orleans. Its packaging featured the comment "sinfully good," with the likeness of actor Vincent Price. This was a potentially winning combination. Where are the cookies today? The excellent product positioning apparently was not backed up with the required funding.

In the beginning, the woman Eve was shopping in the Garden of Eden. As she was browsing through the fresh produce section, a serpent appeared unto her. "Psst, woman!" said the Serpent, "try this." "What is it, O Serpent?" asked Eve. And the Serpent spake unto her, "It is a fruit, as yet unnamed. It grows on the tree of paradise, and it's mostly roughage, so it's good for what aileth you. And, it's a product of nature: eighty-five percent water, vitamins A and C, calcium, thiamin, riboflavin, iron, and niacin." "I've never heard of vitamins," said Eve, "but I don't aileth. I feel great." "Try a bite. Just a bite," urged the Serpent, holding an apple toward her. "It's just what you needeth." "Who needeth anything that's good for them?" retorted Eve, as she headed for the heavenly hash ice cream. "Curses!" spake the Serpent unto himself. "I was sure she'd fall for it." And he slithered away to thinketh. "I know I've got a great product here. Yea, verily, the projected sales figures are out of this world. Maybe my segmentation aileth. Maybe I barketh up the wrong tree. Hmmmeth. Hallelujah! The woman Eve is also a mother. Maybe this product is for kids!" And so the Serpent hired unto him a $100,000-a-year-copywriter. And this copywriter delivered unto the Serpent a terrific advertising slogan: "An apple a day keepeth the doctor away."...And the Serpent saw it was good. The next day, when Eve was shopping, the Serpent appeared unto her again. "Psst, Mom!" said the Serpent, "try this!" "What is it?" asked Eve. "It's a fruit named apple," said the Serpent. "Your kids are gonna love it. It's a sweet, crunchy fun food. Great for afterschool quicketh energy!" "Forget it," said Eve. "Cain and Abel have enough energy. They're killing each other already!" "But," said the Serpent, "it is written: An apple a day keepeth the doctor away." "Who needeth a doctor in paradise?" said Eve. "Besides,

*my kids eateth only peanut butter and jelly."
"Double curses!" hissed the Serpent, and he
crawled off to thinketh again. He thought and he
thought and he thought. And his thinking begat
an idea. He decided to undertaketh giant systematic research. First he spake unto consumers in
Kansas City, Rochester, and Des Moines. And they
spake unto him of their desires. Then he called in
Yankelovich to checketh the demographics. And
Yankelovich spake unto the truth of the Serpent's
findings in a sixteen-volume report. Then he
handed the word of Yankelovich over to a new-
product consulting firm, and he awaited their
suggestions. And those of the firm spake unto him
of the target market and communications thereto,
and the Serpent did as he was told. He painted
the apple bright red. He polished it until it shone
even as the sun. He garnished it with a stem and
a little green leaf. ...And he saw it was good.
Then he placed it in the center of the fruit section
and crawled off to waiteth. The next day, the
woman Eve came byeth pushing her shopping
cart. The beautiful apple caught her eye, and she
spake. "O Serpent," she asked, "what's this?" And
the Serpent knew great joy, and he spake unto her,
"It's something new. It's a tempting dessert. It's a
little sinful, and all natural, and very, very indul-
gent, and loweth in calories and it's called 'Fatal
Apple'. You probably can't afford it." "Sayeth
who?" said Eve, "I'll take a bushel." And lo, the
Serpent and Eve begat positioning, which
dwelleth among us, even unto this day.*

Market Share

Market share is the percentage of a given market that a food producer is said to control. For example, "XYZ Tea Company" may claim a 75 percent share of the market for "imported retail packaged British tea" which means that of all the retail packaged British Tea sold in the U.S., 75 percent is sold by "XYZ Tea Company."

Case In Point

China Bowl Trading Company imported Chinese sauces, flavorings, spices and herbs. The company spent nearly fifteen years in developing its share of the market before selling it to the Swiss firm Estee. The company markets to both the specialty and grocery food trades.

It will be unlikely for you to start out as the product leader in your category; therefore, you should think seriously about not being number two, but rather, becoming a market niche competitor. This is precisely why the specialty food industry works. Why is this? The leading seller of mustard, for example, may have a 30 percent share of the total mustard market, with a ten percent net profit margin. You, on the other hand, could carve out a one to two percent share of the mustard market, with a ten percent net profit margin. The idea is to focus on overall profitability rather than beating the product leader in the market share race.

Market share is generally of little consequence to the entry level marketeer; however, you should know that major food processors seem to "allow" small companies about 1 percent share of a given market before launching a competitive campaign.

General Foods, for example, claims a 38 percent share of the estimated $440 million specialty coffee market. If your new specialty coffee roasting business can sell up to $4 million per year, then you can expect some attention form General Foods. Otherwise, you will face most of your competition from other coffee roasters looking for a niche.

Actually, if you can sell $4 million of roasted coffee, then you might want to submit a "buyout" by a larger company. It has been one way to make a lot of money.

Consumer Attitudes

Purchases of specialty foods have grown to $10 billion per year because of consumer demand for quality. Specialty foods represent affordable luxury. Even in recessions, purchases of many fancy foods tend to remain constant.

In the late 1970's, the United States experienced a consumer backlash to mediocrity. Notably, consumers had begun to take an interest in products with natural ingredients, no preservatives, and no artificial coloring. Purchases of fancy foods were based on considerations of quality and health.

The consumer backlash occasioned the remarkable growth of fine foods throughout the 1980's. All of a sudden, everyone knew about brie. As more products were introduced, and new entrees proliferated, consumers developed a preference for a particular product brand or make. In the specialty food industry, the concept of *brand preference* was just becoming a factor in understanding consumer behavior. There is still plenty of room for experimentation, and, fortunately for new entrepreneurs, consumers appear disposed to continue in that vein.

With the exception of a handful of "transition products," very few specialty food brand preferences have emerged. Those brands that are requested by name include: Heublein's Grey Poupon mustard, Celestial Seasonings herbal beverages, Godiva chocolates, and Häagen-Dazs ice cream.

The specialty food retail business thrives on appealing to the senses. This makes for considerable impulse buying. Some of the most successful products are those sold in retail outlets where shopping is an exciting adventure. There, consumers are surrounded by new aromas and different tastes from sampled products. Products with eye-catching displays and packaging further embellish this experience.

"Sizzle" Considerations For Your Product

❖ Packaging.....upscale

❖ Labeling.......upscale, refined

❖ Ingredients...the best

❖ Size ....appropriate (no "giant economy")

❖ Price.............on the high side (cost of production)

❖ Shape ....upscale, but practical

Consumer attitudes toward specialty foods are influenced by that which is exclusive, new and different.

Once consumers become familiar with a specific product, they will then experiment with other products from the same line. For example, the "Gourmet Line" company's strawberry preserve will be tried. If it is liked, consumers will feel more disposed to try other types of preserves offered by the "Gourmet Line" company. Other producer's products will be tried only if unavailable under the preferred brand. If "Gourmet Line" does not have a blueberry preserve, then consumers may try one from another firm.

Finally, consumer attitudes toward specialty foods are influenced by that which is exclusive, new and different. Products offering something unique will attract consumer interest. As long as these consumers want more new and better foods, there will be a continuing growth potential for new products.

Having said that, the growth of specialty foods in the 1980's occasioned a substantial widening of the traditional specialty food market to include greater distribution through down-market supermarket chains. If the recession of the 1990's intensifies, these supermarkets will look very closely at product turnover and will, doubtless, begin to eliminate a number of the specialty food lines they carry. In turn, the eliminated lines, once the bulwark of gourmet food outlets, will attempt to regain their foothold in those outlets, causing even further fallout in this widely over-assorted industry. Consider olive oil which is presently over-distributed and carried in too many versions by too many supermarkets. The specialty food market, acting like a contracting accordion, may have insufficient room to accommodate these and many other products currently in distribution.

Competition

With whom will you compete? Aside from every other food producer, you will find your direct competition from others with similar products. Competition from other makers of "condiments," for example, will occur when the consumer chooses their product instead of yours.

You will be competing for shelf space, too. There is a finite amount of shelving, and a growing number of products for the retailer to select. Fortunately, there is a lot of product movement. Product life cycles end, and products move to larger, down market (grocery) distribution. As this occurs, specialty food stores demand products that will replace those that moved to supermarket shelves.

You will be competing for the "scarce dollar." Consumers must want to spend more for your fancy sauce, instead of a less expensive grocery-grade catsup. Consumers have differing perceptions of different products. Many are impulsive—they like the packaging, for example. Choices as to how to spend limited discretionary income are difficult to make. Products that impart the most "sizzle" will attract the most scarce dollars.

In his book, *The Business Planning Guide*, David Bangs considers the following questions in analyzing competition: Who are your five major competitors? How is their business steady, increasing or decreasing? How are their products similar and dissimilar to yours? What have you learned about their operation? How will your product be better than theirs?

High Volume Versus Lower Volume-High Margin

A margin is the amount of money (profit) charged above the actual cost of the product. The specialty food trade consists of products that are characterized by low sales volumes and high profit margins. Profit percentages are higher in the specialty food industry than they are in the grocery industry.

The specialty food retailer will normally take a forty to fifty percent profit *margin*; whereas, the grocery store/supermarket uses *mark ups* of three to twenty percent on most staple groceries. In some cases, supermarkets will use twenty to forty percent profit margins for certain fast turnover items, such as bottled water, delicatessen products and other products requiring service personnel.

The reasoning behind this difference in profits is two-fold: (1) *Industry tradition* suggests that specialty food marketers determine their profits by computing them as a percentage of product sales, rather than adding a percentage to product cost. (2) *Product turnover.* Retailers need to achieve a targeted contribution (sales X margins) from space used. The specialty food retailer is likely to move ten jars of fancy preserves in a day. By comparison, the grocer may move several *dozen* jars of jam in the same period. Therefore, because it costs more to carry the fancy preserves, the specialty food retailer must sell the product at a higher profit margin. A further explanation of the difference between "mark ups" and "margins" will appear later in this chapter under the heading, "Pricing the Product."

Cases In Point

A "bird's-eye" view of life in specialty food marketing: Condiments, mustard, tortilla chips, gourmet nuts, sauces, mixes, dressings, marinades, etc. Generally developed by persons with free time, lots of energy, creativity, and little money. Bankrolled by spouse and friends. Spend two to three years developing and packaging the product. Exhibit at trade shows in usually shared booths. Conduct demonstrations at retail stores. Lots of first-time sales, but few repeat orders. At third or fourth year, begin to realize this may not be their salvation. Then, they either take what they have learned, work up a business plan, and obtain financing, or go home and lick their wounds.

GUIDELINES FOR SUCCESS
Product Development
(With thanks to Daniel Best, Technical Director, *Prepared Foods* magazine)

Network

Contact others in the supplier community. Also, contact independent labs, universities and reputable free-lance product developers.

Know your customer

Be "market-oriented" rather than "product-oriented." Region, ethnicity and eating occasion can all affect perceptions of quality. Don't equate your taste preferences with those of your customers.

Identify product traits

Begin by defining all consumer-relevant product features in advance of development. Engineer the desirable attributes into the product (packaging, color, flavor, etc.), rather than defining product attributes after product design. Consumer test to determine how closely product variables match consumer needs and perception. Refine to reflect consumer reaction.

Manage your resources

You must manage by focus and flexibility. New products require time, labor and capital. Investing in highly-specialized processing systems closely married to a single product or product line is risky and expensive. Think long term. Apply processing systems that will be applicable beyond the immediate project requirements. However, by spreading your labor resources over a wide range of product development, you minimize the risk of generating both failures and superstars.

Maintain product quality

A long series of minute cost reductions will not reduce perceptions of quality in consumer testing. But, the end result will be compounded, and the overall quality of the product will suffer.

Control your costs

If your costs come in too high, then reexamine the basic factors. Are your ingredients priced too high, and are lower-cost sources available? Are alternative processing methods available? Can you find other market segments to capitalize on, and consequently increase volume projections? Was the projected price for the product too low?

Commit for the long term

Failure to commit can result in constantly changing signals and erratic funding. Focus on your strategic objectives and tenaciously commit to their long term achievement. However, know when to cut your losses and pursue alternatives.

Pay heed to the time factor

Timing is critical. Too soon, and your product may not be ready. Too late, and someone else will be in the market with the same product.

Tactics and strategy

Do not mistake tactics for strategy. Excessive focus on tactics can leave you struggling for strategies to fit. Tactics are the processes employed to achieve your objectives. Your objectives are your marketing and financial goals. Strategies combine tactics to achieve objectives.

Manage by confrontation

Risk avoidance can become the path of least resistance when there is no freedom to fail. In your case, management by avoidance will stop you dead in your tracks. You simply cannot avoid making the complex and success threatening decisions associated with specialty food marketing.

PRODUCING THE PRODUCT

Because this is a marketing guide, no attempt is made to tell you how to produce your product. We will devote some attention to product selection, packaging and labeling, and will offer a partial listing of companies that can package and help you produce your product. (Appendix C.)

You must make a clear connection between your product development efforts on the one hand, and the market and consumer demand on the other. The U.S. Food, Drug, and Cosmetic Act is very specific as to sanitation requirements. You should ask the Food and Drug Administration to provide you with a copy of the Current Good Manufacturing Practice Regulations. These regulations set forth the requirements for establishing and maintaining sanitary conditions.

In addition to federal regulations, each state has special requirements for inspecting and certifying food producing facilities. If your initial production effort will occur in your own kitchen facility (separate from your "home" kitchen), then have it inspected and certified by your local food regulating agency.

Product Liability
Many distributors will ask you to provide them with a current certificate of product liability insurance coverage. They will request that the certificate name them as an additional insured, to be included under "Broad Form Vendor's" coverage.

Be prepared to pay a hefty premium. Lately, when courts in the United States have found in favor of plaintiffs, they have awarded sums that have exceeded existing levels of defendant's liability coverage. As a result, coverage can be difficult to find and expensive to maintain.

If you are setting up your own manufacturing facility, you will have to pay for workmen's compensation insurance, as well as offer some sort of group medical insurance to your employees. Check with your insurance agent for guidance about the types of insurance coverage best suited for your operation.

GUIDELINES FOR SUCCESS
Government Regulations

Process	Responsible Agency
Business Organization	State and local departments of economic affairs. Application depends on the type of organization (corporation, proprietorship, etc.) you elect.
Production	State Health Agencies. Sanitary certification, inspection laws.
Labeling	U.S. Food and Drug Administration. U.S. Customs (if you are marketing an imported product). Chapter 21 of U.S. Code of Federal Regulations includes the labeling laws. Required nutritional statement laws go into effect in 1993.
Labor	Internal Revenue Service and state and local revenue agencies. Payment of FICA, withholding tax, and workmens' compensation.
Tax	Internal Revenue Service and state and local revenue agencies. For quarterly and annual income tax payments and procedures.
Distribution	Some states require registration of your products before they can be sold in that state. A well-known example of this is the Pennsylvania law requiring all baked products to be registered.

PACKAGING THE PRODUCT

Packaging is the single most important element in the decision to purchase a new specialty food product. Packaging type and design are paramount to success in the specialty food trade.

Types of Packaging
The packaging you select will depend on the product. For example, different merchandising is re-

quired for bulk fancy foods, such as snacks and confections. However, if you have alternative packaging types to consider, then you should be aware of the impact some packages have over others. Witness the shape of the Perrier bottle. Packaging encompasses consumer perceptions, as well as practical considerations.

Glass containers are used because the product can be seen and there is no tin taste; whereas, canned (tinned) products are generally restricted to soups, pâtés, caviar and most loose teas. Most consumers tend to prefer products in jars, rather than cans, despite a can's practicality.

Some of the fanciest packaging available is also the most expensive. At first, you will probably have minimum production "runs," so you will not want to purchase thousands of empty jars, boxes, or other containers. The objective is to limit your initial costs, regardless of the economies of scale associated with large volume purchases. There is little point in ordering a thousand jars and a thousand labels if you are not sure of selling a thousand units of your product.

Packaging types for specialty food products are many and varied. You can select from among readily obtainable containers made of cardboard, plastic, wood, cellophane, glass and metal. Try to find a good looking and reasonably priced container. Do not try to pack your product in an odd-shaped container. As a rule, your product must be able to fit and stack on standard store shelves. It is wise to start with stock items (such as jars and lids) rather than design special molds, etc.

Competition's Packaging

It will serve your purpose to review products now on the shelves of specialty food stores. It stands to reason that, generally, you should package your product in a container type that is similar to those on the shelves.

Case In Point

Market Square Food Company developed a beautifully designed line of specialty foods, all packaged in containers depicting wildlife and water fowl paintings by noted artist James Lockhart. The company initially centered on sales to specialty food and department stores. Competition, especially with its lines of wild rice, vinegar, and olive oils, caused it to eventually re-focus its efforts by targeting the gift trade. Today, it sells its snack mixes, confections and candy exclusively through "food reps" to the gift trade.

This comes under the heading of "you can't knock success." It does not mean that your creative urges should be constrained, just that the consequent costs and requirements for educating consumers about your unique package may not be worth the expense.

Elements of Great Packaging

Aside from clearly conveying its contents, great packaging will cause your product to stand out from others. It will demand consumer attention and create interest in the product.

Visit several of your local gourmet food stores, and attend the next International Fancy Food and Confection Show to see examples of great packaging. The Fancy Food Show has a special display called: "Focused Exhibits." It offers you the opportunity to see hundreds of new products, gift products, and foodservice products away from the producer's show booth. And it will provide you with a terrific chance to compare differing packaging styles.

Contract Packaging

Co-packers are food processing companies that either have excess packing capacity, or are specifically devoted to packing other people's products. Their capabilities vary and some can only pack tinned (canned) products, while others can only package dry, non-perishable products.

You may want to seek assistance in formulating and packing your product. See the comments that follow and the listing of co-packers in Appendix C. Check with industry sources in your state, especially your state's business development agency, for assistance.

The complexities of moving a product from conception to market can be overwhelming even to experienced entrepreneurs. Developing networking relationships with reliable co-packers will permit the small businessperson to achieve maximum utiliza-

Case In Point

Truzzolino Food Products, long a mainstay of canned foods in Montana, retained the Chicago-based design firm Power Packaging to redesign its line of canned Mexican-style tamales (almost a cult food in certain parts of Montana), and its gourmet chile. The result was a very fancy looking canned tamale. Despite making many of the right moves, the line never caught on nationally, and Truzzolino returned to its co-packing and regional food marketing activities.

tion of physical and financial resources—and save time.

Working with co-packers allows the business owner to call the shots while drawing on various team members to perform, when needed, on a fee-for-service basis.

When you approach co-packers, be prepared to present your product and your needs clearly and concisely. You will be received best if you deal efficiently without wasting their time or yours. Be open in discussing your needs and their costs.

The major areas of co-packer operation include Basic Product Development Services, Food Processing Services, and Food Packaging Services. Each is described below (with thanks to John Darack, of the Dirigo Corporation).

Basic Product Development Services - These are often available from ingredient suppliers, such as seasoning manufacturers. Such service providers perform an important function by helping you convert at-home or menu recipes to a manufacturable form. Then, dry ingredients, and often several "wet" ones such as fresh vegetables, liquid sauces, condiments, meats, fats, and so forth, can be formulated into one specialized ingredient package. The resulting product can either be sold as an easy-prep—as is—item, or sent to a processor to be converted into a canned or jarred finished product.

Using basic product development services accomplishes several benefits:

◆ Quality Control - The blender guarantees that agreed upon specifications for the product will be met.

Cost Saving Hints

Negotiate small initial production runs. Your unit costs might be higher, but you won't be saddled with thousands of a slow-moving inventory. Limit initial production costs by using readily available stock items.

- Inventory Control - Only one item needs to be tracked, rather than several.
- Recipe Protection - The blender signs a contract in which your recipe is kept confidential. Finished product producers know only to add the simple liquids to a preweighed unit of ingredients.
- Uniformity of Finished Product - All ingredients are pre-weighed and batched. Opportunities for errors in production are eliminated.
- Price Stabilization and Purchasing Power - The blender has the ability to purchase in large quantities from reliable and established sources. Cost averaging and unitized pricing eliminate being at the mercy of market fluctuations. You will know your costs over longer price periods.
- Networking - You will be "plugged in" to an existing array of related services, such as analytical laboratories, packagers, processors, marketers and distributors that may not be otherwise available to the public.

Food Processing Services - After having your recipe converted into manufacturable form, you can bring your ingredient package and conversion recipe to a food processor. Be prepared to discuss the preparation of your finished product to your specifications. Liquid ingredients, process parameters, packaging, labeling, shelf life testing, and possibly even distribution are topics you should address.

Be ready to deal with some practical limitations such as larger or smaller batch proportions, limited size or shaped containers, production scheduling, and ingredients availability (seasonally or otherwise).

Find the best fit—don't go to a large producer for small batch production. Conversely, be sure the processor has the capacity to accommodate your growth.

Food Packaging Services—If yours is a dry product, then find a packaging company that has the right equipment to make your ideal package. As with a processor, the right fit must be found. There are companies that specialize only in contract packaging.

Opportunities can also be found at plants that package products in similar type materials to yours, and which would like to utilize down-time profitably. Good deals can be made here.

Co-Packer Benefits

Successful co-packing can provide you with significant benefit and cost savings, among which are:

◆ Elimination of capital costs - no plant to build or equipment to purchase.
◆ Utilization of well seasoned experts - solving problems which overwhelm you are a part of their daily routine.
◆ Compliance - undergo the amazingly complex process of meeting federal, state and local regulations.
◆ Product uniformity.
◆ Purchasing power.
◆ Networking.
◆ Technical services - often at cost, or low cost.
◆ Marketing assistance.
◆ Distribution.

Case In Point

About working with co-packers, Boston-based Dirigo Corporation Technical Director John Darack has this to say: "Being in business should be a rewarding experience. Don't fall into the trap of thinking you can do it all. Build and work with the team of experts who will remove the obstacles on your road to success."

Examples of Products with Great Packaging

Category	Product (s)	Producer (s)
Condiment/Sauce	Vermont Honey with Lemon	The Herb Patch
Confection	Excellence Almond Creme, Meringue & Swiss Chocolate Cookies	Kambly
Dressings/Marinades	Various	The Cook's Classic and The Alder Market lines
Bagged Snack	Seasoned Pretzels	East Shore Products
Baked Goods	Scones	Titterington's Olde English Bake Shop
Jam/Preserve	Various	Elsenham Preserves
Entree	Chicken Breast Parisienne	Vivian's Home Gourmet
Packaged Produce	Various	Epicurean Herbs
Sparkling Water	Icelandia Water	Icelandia Water Corp
Smoked Fish	Gourmet Smoked Trout Fillets	Silver Creek Farms

Packaging Considerations

In selecting the container and the means of packaging, review government regulations that may apply. For example, the state of California requires honey to be sold in eight-ounce and sixteen-ounce containers. Any other size is viewed as potentially misleading to consumers.

Most big cities have glass suppliers, for example, and it is worthwhile to visit their showrooms, obtain their catalogs, and try your product in sample containers before making any final decision.

Increasing use of tamper-resistant seals suggests that you should consider employing such a device on your product's container. Also, if you want to add a consumer information neck tag to help educate the specialty food consumer about the benefits of your product, then this should be planned before you make your final packaging decision.

If you plan to sell to supermarkets, then consider such elements as supermarket shelf depth and height. If your product is packaged in a container that exceeds the shelf height, then it will be placed on the top shelf, out of direct eye contact. This applies to the number of facings that can be accommodated. If the product is too wide, then it will take up more than one facing per product. This may limit the amount of space that the store will authorize for your product or product line.

Outer Containers

The outer container is the shipping container. The most common outer container is a strong cardboard carton capable of holding one dozen units of your product. Because you will be making use of such pick up and delivery services as United Parcel Service, make certain that the outer container can withstand the rather substantial punishment shipments often encounter. A master pack capable of withstanding a 200 pound test, with a size of eighteen inches square will fit nicely on a pallet, for example, and make for easier and more cost effective shipping.

Retailers are asking for products in smaller outer packages. Generally, one dozen products per outer package is sufficient; however, if you can break down the pack to two packs of six, for example, you will find retailers more willing to try your product. Also, your suppliers can provide glass jars in twelve-pack cartons that you can reuse once the jars have been filled. Often, these outer packs can be put into master cartons containing two by twelve by unit (one master carton with two inner cartons of twelve

Size Points

Cost: select best for your budget.
Selling Price: cost to consumer can influence container size selected.
Usage (repeat sales): a 16-ounce jar may move once a month; whereas, an 8-ounce jar may move three or more times a week!
Shipping Containers: should hold no more than one dozen units.

jars each), or four by six units (master carton with four inner cartons of six jars each).

You may want to purchase mailing containers that can be used for individual direct sales and for shipping samples to prospective buyers. These can be sold to retailers when your product has a gift potential, allowing the consumer to have the retailer mail it to the gift recipient.

Other packaging considerations include the use of corrugated cartons, bubble wrap, filler materials, and associated equipment such as wrapping tape and tape guns. There are numerous sources for these, and almost any manufacturer or co-packer will be able to provide you with the name of a packing materials supplier.

GUIDELINES FOR SUCCESS
Packaging

Describe packaging type used by your competition (jar, can, plastic container, etc.):

Your anticipated product package type (should be similar type to competition):

Is it a stock item, or does it require special order? (check with suppliers):

Minimum order for stock item (supplier requirements):

Minimum production run for special order (supplier requirements):

Special handling required (example: cardboard to be lithographed, or sticker labeled?):

Special shipping containers required (box, glass, etc.):

Are co-packers available to package for you? (see partial listing in Appendix C):

Does your package design conform to federal and local regulations? (example: honey in California cannot be put into a 12 oz jar - need 8 or 16 oz):

Is your package size consistent with consumer demand? (price will have an impact):

Does the outer container hold no more than one dozen of your product? (unofficial industry standard):

LABELING THE PRODUCT

All labels must conform to government regulations. Even so, you will have a wide choice. Remember, your label is a crucial element in attracting consumers. It must convey the nature of your product, as well as the "sense" of affordable luxury.

At first, you should consider some type of pressure-sensitive adhesive label that can be designed and printed in small batches. Compare the costs of applying labels by hand and by machine. After you get the product up-and-running, you can have your labels printed in quantity. As with packaging, the color and style of your label will be important in attracting consumers. Avoid the "supermarket look" with its reliance on bold lettering and lots of primary colors. The same company that packs your product will be able to help you have it labeled. Otherwise, you can hire labor to hand-label the product until your volume warrants automated labeling.

Uniform Product Code

This is an optic-readable symbol that can be affixed to your product label. The UPC symbol allows use of automated check out machines and conforms more readily to other products on the shelves. As items are presented to the checker, they are passed over an optical scanner that decodes the UPC symbol and transmits this information to a computer. The computer stores price and other information on all items carried in the store. It transmits back to the checkstand the item's price and description, which are then displayed to the customer and printed on the customer receipt.

The UPC code is an eleven-digit, all numeric code that will identify the product. The code consists of a five-digit manufacturer identification number and a five-digit item code number. The eleventh digit is a scanner-readable check digit. At this writing, UPC codes are not required by all distributors;

Example of a UPC code

however, they are becoming more evident as food producers and distributors recognize the increasing influence the large grocery chains have in specialty food distribution. These chains tend to require UPC coding.

If you anticipate ever having your product on a supermarket shelf, it is less expensive and more efficient to have your initial label carry the UPC. In this manner, you will save labor by not having to affix it separately. Information regarding UPC allocation may be obtained from the Uniform Product Code Council (reference Appendix M).

F. D. A. Labeling Requirements

Aside from your desire to impart ingredient information to the consumer, the U.S. Food and Drug Administration enforces label ingredient legislation. The laws require that ingredients be stated clearly, and in accordance with the regulation. A net weight statement is also required. In this connection, the American Technology Pre-eminence Act, that amends the Fair Packaging and Labeling Act, will require all packaging and labeling to use metric measurements of net quantity. The use of ounces and pounds would become optional. Compliance is re-

The Nutritional Labeling and Education Act

(Final Interpretation Pending)
Exceptions to the requirement for nutritional labeling include coffee, tea and spice, containers too small to carry a nutritional label, and producers whose total annual revenues are less than $500,000.

Note: *As of this writing, the Nutritional Labeling and Education Act (NLEA) of 1990 is scheduled to take effect in May 1993. Many of its current provisions are still being interpreted by the F.D.A. Why is this important? Because, a total work-up on a single sample compliance with the NLEA by a food laboratory can cost more than $600!*

quired as of February 14, 1994. Furthermore, the law is very specific about the nutritional claims that can be made for any food product. Claims as to health, purity, low-sodium, and the like must be made in no uncertain terms. The code specifies what wording is permitted, and what wording is proscribed.

The FDA has promulgated new labeling regulations (Public Law 101-535) that will require practically every food to have nutritional labeling. Regulations as to cholesterol content, and serving sizes are also being issued. Finally, there is some confusion as to which laws will take precedence when federal and state requirements differ. It will be necessary for you to check Chapter 21 of the Code of Federal Regulations, available from your local Government Printing Office, (or from the Superintendent of Documents, Government Printing Office, Washington, DC) to determine the requirements as they pertain to your ingredient statements.

There are regulations governing the physical aspects as well. Certain information has to be placed on certain parts of the label, and the lettering size has to be in specific relation to the overall size of the label, or "principal display panel."

What if you goof? The Food and Drug Administration will not officially approve your label; however, your local compliance branch will provide comment on the manner with which the label conforms to the regulations. If you sell the product with incorrect labeling, expect the FDA to enforce the law at the store level. It can cause all the product to be removed from the store shelves.

Labeling Considerations

One of your greater setbacks can occur when you recognize that your beautiful labels might be "ruined" by the label requirements. You must have a net weight statement placed in the lower third of the principal display panel, for example. If you know of this requirement beforehand, then you can save time and money by designing your original labels to allow for the legal statements. There are many ways of retaining your artistic statement while complying with the law. Your labels should have eye appeal, be informative and legal. Remember that one of the key elements of a specialty food product is its presentation.

Labels offer more than practical and aesthetic forms of expression. They should be used to convey your sales message. Consider including usage instructions, cooking directions, recipe tips, and the like.

The front label (or principal display panel) is used for a different purpose than the side and rear labels. The front is the "tickler" that attracts consumer attention. The side and rear may include additional messages regarding the product use, such as those mentioned above, or convey a message about other elements of your product. Remember the success of the "notes to consumers" on the cartons of Celestial Seasonings Herbal Tea.

GUIDELINES FOR SUCCESS
Labeling the Product

❖ Will you do the labeling yourself?

❖ Can labeling be completed by a contract labeler?

❖ Can your initial label be produced in a limited quantity?

❖ Does your label conform with local and federal regulations? (Code of Federal Regulations, Chapter 21.)

❖ Will your label contain a nutritional statement? (Not required if total annual sales will be under $500,000.)

❖ Is your label consistent with that of an upscale product? Does it impart a sense of high quality?

❖ Does your label stand out from your competition? (Or, is it the same old, same old?)

❖ Does your label give history of company, recipe tips, or other "selling" information?

❖ Describe how your label attracts consumer interest.

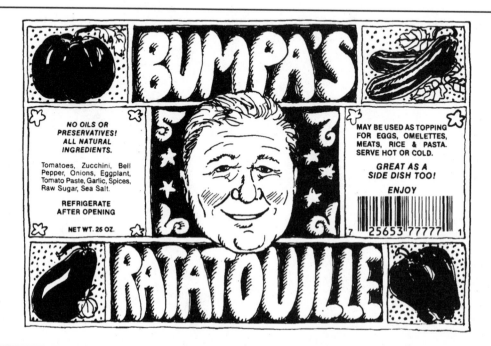

PRICING THE PRODUCT

Earlier in this chapter I addressed the desirability of finding a market niche. Rather than concentrating on beating the product leader for market share, I suggested a goal of one percent to two percent market share with a ten percent net profit margin. In striving for this goal, I underscored the use of margins instead of mark ups (cost plus profit). When using margins, profit is calculated on selling price. The specialty food industry uses margins instead of mark ups to develop prices. The following examples will illustrate the difference.

Mark Up

The unit cost of your peppercorn breadsticks is $1.00. If you were to use a forty percent *mark up*, your selling price would be $1.40. To determine your selling price, multiply the $1.00 by 1.40 ($1.00 X 1.40 = $1.40).

Margin

The unit cost of your peppercorn breadsticks is $1.00 and you decide to use a forty percent gross profit *margin*. Your selling price will be $1.67. To determine your selling price, subtract .40 from 1.00 and divide the $1.00 cost by .60 (1.00 -.40 =.60. $1.00 divided by .60 = $1.67).

The different selling prices of $1.40 and $1.67 occur when you use a mark up versus a margin. The mark up is cost plus profit; whereas, the margin is calculated on selling price less profit. Another example: Your honey mustard cost is $1.63. A forty percent mark up= $2.28 selling price. A forty percent margin = $2.72 selling price.

Cost Accounting

This involves computing all your costs, adding your profit, and the profit margins taken by distributors and retailers, to reach a consumer price. No matter what the costs, if your price to the consumer is greater than that of the competition, you will face substantial consumer resistance. It is for this reason that I recommend starting with your competitor's price, and working backward through the various profit margins to your product costs (unless you have that "one-in-a-million" product for which the world has been waiting. In that case, demand will be considered "elastic" and you will have more leeway).

You may use either a cost-plus or market-set pricing method. The former begins from the bottom up, while the latter works backwards from the consumer price to your product cost. My recommendation is to use the latter.

First, establish a consumer price (use your competitor's price as a reference). That will enable you to determine your gross profit after the retailer and distributor margins are deducted. Then, determine if your costs and profit margin yield a price significantly different from your competition.Some of your strategic thinking can be assisted by applying a break-even analysis that will help you determine the price range available for your product. A break-even analysis will let you know at what point your dollar or unit sales will meet your total dollar or unit costs. Any revenue generated above the break-even point is profit—below it is loss. Detailed discussions of break-even analyses appear in almost all of the business management books on the market. David Bangs' *The Business Planning Guide*, (available from Upstart Publishing, 800-235-8866) contains a complete explanation of the topic.

Selected Cost Factors

Ingredients   Cost of contents of your product.

Packaging   Cost of outer package, the reinforced cardboard carton.

Production   Labor and materials used in getting the ingredients into the containers.

Containers   The jars, boxes or cans used to hold your product.

Labeling   Design, artwork, mechanicals, printing, and affixing costs.

Selling   Cost of making sales calls.

Promotion   Special events, trade shows, in-store demonstrations.

Advertising   Sales literature, trade journals and related media costs.

Administration   Cost of running your "office," includes legal, accounting, etc.

Overhead   Regular costs of running the business that you will incur whether or not anything is produced or sold. Some include rent, utilities, upkeep, and taxes.

Draw   Your salary. Divide your annual gross salary requirements by 260 (average number of work days per year) to get a realistic assessment of your daily pay. Divide that by eight for the hourly version. Even though you probably will not take a draw, knowing this amount will be helpful in your break-even analysis.

Delivered Price Versus Exwarehouse Cost

Depending on the circumstances, some transactions will require that you include freight charges in your pricing for a "delivered price." Others will allow you to ship freight collect, or with the freight charges added to the invoice.

Exwarehouse cost is the cost of the product (plus freight-in if you are importing) plus the cost of storage and handling. Your exwarehouse cost plus profit margin yields your price to the retailer. In these examples, we will use a gross profit margin of forty percent, which is consistent with profit margins used by many food processors. In our examples, prices do not include freight, and they are called F.O.B. (Free On Board). Freight will be "collect," or added to your invoice to be paid by the buyer.

Your gross profit margin will include administration costs, and sales and marketing costs (broker commissions, promotion, reserve for bad debts, advertising, and the like). Your gross profit margin will have to cover all of these costs. You should aim for a net profit of at least ten percent. (See the suggested pricing formulas that follow.)

Suggested Pricing Formula for Sales to Distributors

Formula: $D = E /(100\% - P)$
> where,
> D = Price to distributor,
> E = Exwarehouse cost per unit,
> P = Gross profit margin.

Example: E = $2.25 (product cost of $2.20 plus 5 cents for storage and handling)

> P = 20%

Process:
D = E/ (100% - 20%). Then $2.25/ 80% = $2.81 per unit. Your gross profit would be $ .56 ($2.81 less $2.25) for a 20% profit margin. Broker commission is 5% ($. 14) and will be deducted from the profit margin.

Most retailers in the specialty food industry work on at least a forty percent margin. They will divide the cost to them from the distributor (or from you for a direct sale) by 60 to arrive at their price to the consumer.

Suggested Pricing Formula
for Sales to Retailers

Formula: R = E/ (100% - P)
    where,
    R = Price to retailer,
    E = Exwarehouse cost per unit,
    P = Gross profit margin.

Example: E = $2.25 (product cost of $2.20 plus 5 cents for storage and handling)

    P = 40%

Process:
    R = E/ (100% - 40%). Then $2.25/ 60% = $3.75 per unit. Your gross profit would be $1.50 ($3.75 less $2.25), for a 40% profit margin. This is before broker commission (10%). In this example, the price to the consumer will be $6.25 (retailer price of $3.75/ 60% = $6.25).

You may find that the resulting consumer price of $6.25, in the example, is competitive for your eight-ounce jar of cooking sauce. But, if you are selling a one-ounce packet of dill dip mix, then the product will be above the "price point" for its category, and you will probably encounter stiff consumer resistance.

Broker Commissions

Your gross profit margin should include, right from the beginning, the broker commission percentage. This will range from five to fifteen percent, depending on the type of broker used. Brokers who sell to chain stores, independent wholesalers, and distributors will require a five percent commission. Sales via brokers to department stores, retailers, and gift shops will be commissioned at ten percent. Brokers who have their own showrooms, and who call on retail gift and food stores, will require a fifteen percent commission.

LARRY FORGIONE'S
NO SUGAR ADDED
CORN RELISH
A deliciously savory relish developed by Chef Forgione at "An American Place" Restaurant in New York City.
Not a reduced calorie food.
Please refrigerate after opening.
AMERICAN SPOON FOODS ®
NET WEIGHT 9 OZ

Distributor Margins

The distributor will add a profit margin to your distributor price, usually a minimum of 25% (divide the distributor cost by 75), to arrive at the distributor's price to the retailer.

Pricing Flow Example

Following is a pricing flow example from consumer price back through retailer, distributor to your exwarehouse cost.

Price to consumer		$6.25
Less 40%	X	60
Equals cost to retailer		3.75
Price to retailer		$3.75
Less 25%	X	75
Equals cost to distributor		2.81
Price to distributor		$2.81
Less 20%	X	80
Equals your exwarehouse cost		2.25

Customary broker commissions for sales direct to retailer = 10% ($ .38 in the above example). For sales to a distributor the commission = 5% ($ .14 in the above example). You will use the same price to the retailer, regardless of whether or not you sell to a distributor. Sales to retailers will entail less volume, but you will make more in profit (forty percent gross profit before broker commission).

Bear in mind the concept of price points, or thresholds, beyond which it would be imprudent to price your product. These price points are found usually just under the two, three, four, five, and up to ten dollar figures. If your price is $4.09, for example, you may want to consider lowering it to $3.99 or $3.95 in order to overcome buyer objections.

The margins and discounts in the above examples are representative of specialty food trade margins and discounts. There are many variations to these, depending on the product, market, season and so forth.

You should prepare two separate price sheets, one for the retailer and one for the distributor.

Break-Even Analysis

Some of your strategic thinking can be assisted by applying a break-even analysis that will help you determine the price range available for your product. A break-even analysis will let you know at what point your dollar or unit sales will meet your total dollar or unit costs. Any revenue generated above the break-even point is profit—below it is loss.

Detailed discussions of break-even analyses appear in almost all of the business management books on the market. David Bangs' *The Business Planning Guide* is the source of the following explanation on the topic:

The break-even point can be calculated by the following formula:

$$S = FC + VC$$

where

S   =   Break-even level of sales in dollars,
FC =   Fixed costs in dollars, and
VC =   Variable costs in dollars.

Fixed costs remain constant regardless of sales volume (at least until your sales volume grows so much as to require capital improvements, such as new buildings, etc.). They are the costs that must be met even if you make no sales. Fixed costs include overhead (rent, administrative, salaries, taxes, benefits, etc.) and depreciation, amortization and interest.

Variable costs are connected to sales volume. They include cost of goods sold (beginning inventory plus freight-in, warehousing, variable labor, broker commissions, etc. less ending inventory).

To calculate the break-even point in the absence of your total variable costs, use the following variation:

$$S = FC/GM$$

where

GM =   Gross margin (profit) expressed as a percentage of sales.

Replace the dollar figures with unit figures if you want to determine the break-even point in units produced instead of dollars earned.

Sample Break-Even Analysis

Total Sales	=	$216,000
Costs of Goods Sold	=	158,320
Gross Margin	=	57,680

Gross Margin/Total Sales = GM%

Fixed Costs $\quad$ FC = $60,570

Gross Margin $\quad$ GM = (57,680/216,000) = 26.7%

Thus, break-even sales
$$= S = FC/GM$$
$$= (\$60,570/.267)$$
$$= \$226,854/year.$$

On a monthly basis, $\qquad$ S = $18,905

If sales are projected at a total of $216,000 for the first year, you will not make a profit—but since you know what you are apt to face, you will be able to plan ahead to finance your business properly.

This pictorial representation of break-even points is a handy way to make objectives more tangible than the usual "$20,000 a month" kind of goal. It can be very illuminating (or daunting) to post your break-even projections, then trace out—in some vivid color on a monthly basis—how near to the projection you have come.

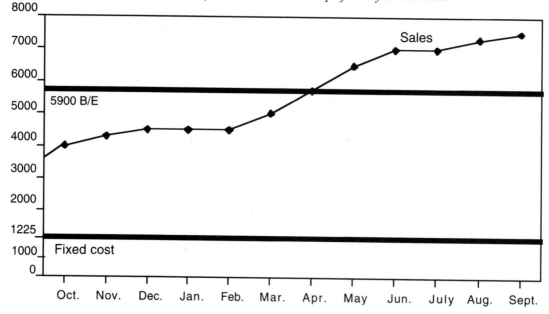

You can also use break-even charts to measure progress towards annual profit goals. Suppose a $12,000 profit the first year. What sales would be needed?

S = (FC + Profit)/GM

where Profit = $12,000;

S = ($60,570 + 12,000)/.267 = $271,797/year
or $22,650/month.

Graphically:

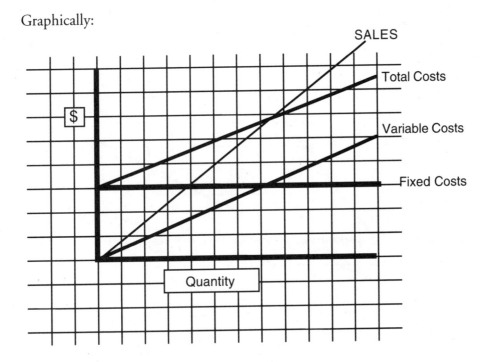

Anytime you can help your employees visualize progress towards a goal, you benefit. Break-even charts are useful for more than financial planning purposes. Once you have calculated break-even sales, you may find it very helpful to break the sales down in terms of customers needed—as a reality check, this can keep you from making overly optimistic projections.

Break-even analysis may also be represented pictorially. The diagramming helps establish forecasts, budgets and projections. Using a chart lets you substitute different combinations of numbers to obtain a rough estimate of their effect on your business.

A helpful technique is to make Worst Case, Best Case, and Most Probable Case Assumptions, chart them to see how soon they cover fixed costs, and then derive more accurate figures by applying the various formulas and kinds of thinking displayed below. This is of particular value if you are thinking of making a capital investment and want a quick picture of the relative merits of buying or leasing.

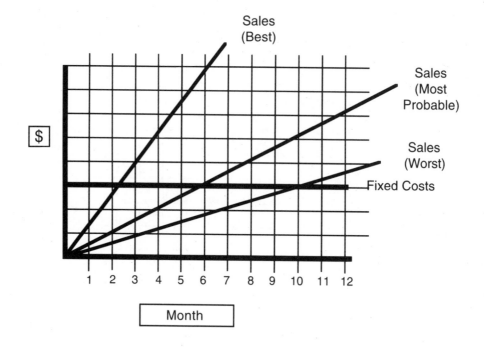

UNDERSTANDING TERMS

Terms are the arrangements for shipping and payment that you establish with your customer. Include your terms on your price lists. An important element of your statement of terms is the establishment of a clear credit policy, from which you should try not to deviate. Among the forms of such a policy are the following:

Terms of Payment: Either F.O.B. your warehouse, or delivered, with entire invoice amount due in 30 days.

Early Payment Discount: Offer either a one or two percent discount for payment made within ten days.

Line of Credit: Inquire of customer's credit references to determine just how much you should allow. Consider withholding shipment if there is an open invoice, or no more than two open invoices within the credit limit.

F.O.B. (Free On Board): F.O.B. warehouse, or delivered, establishes who pays the freight, and when title passes to the customer. If your terms are F.O.B., your warehouse, then the customer pays the freight and takes title to the merchandise when it leaves your warehouse. This means that the customer will be responsible for taking up the issue of any damaged or missing cases with the shipping company. He/she cannot deduct the missing or lost merchandise from your invoice.

If your terms are F.O.B. customer location, or prepaid, then you must seek recourse with the shipping company in the event merchandise is missing on delivery or is damaged enroute. Title passes to the customer when merchandise is delivered, signed for and in good condition.

Suggested terms: To distributors and large volume purchasers: C.O.D., until credit is approved, then

Invoicing Hints

Do not print up thousands of invoice forms! Use your invoices as sales tools. From time-to-time, add a special deal to your invoices to retailers. Many of the retail buyers are also the payers. Offer them a special "re-order deal" that they can send in with their payments—the deal to be billed later.

2%/10 days, Net 30 days, delivered. (This means that the purchaser may deduct 2% from the net invoice amount if paid in full within ten days. Otherwise, the total is due in 30 days.)

To retailers: C.O.D., until credit is approved, then Net 30 days, F.O.B. warehouse.

Include the comment: "Prices subject to change without notice," on price lists and invoices.

Credit

Your ability to assess effectively your buyer's integrity will influence the procedures you undertake to evaluate "credit worthiness." Do not become overly impressed by buyers from high visibility/high prestige outlets. Rarely do these companies pay according to your terms.

The process: Request prospective buyers to provide you with three trade references and one bank reference. Ask for contact names and telephone numbers because some references will release this type of credit information over the telephone, and this will save time. You can expect that the credit checking procedure will take about three to four weeks, which is why I recommend shipping C.O.D. for the first order.

In the specialty food industry, most credit arrangements consist of the following:

Open Account: This means that you are satisfied with the "credit worthiness" of your customer, and that you ship on receipt of orders on your usual terms, wherein payment is due at the end of the 30 day period. Note that the specialty food industry tends to interpret payment terms of NET 30 days, for example, as starting on the day the merchandise is received, rather than on the date of the invoice, or ship date.

C.O.D.: "Cash on delivery" is generally used with first-time customers, until their credit is approved. C.O.D. terms may also be used on request by some small retailers who prefer it to the requirements for accounts payable bookkeeping.

You request the trucking company to collect a specified amount, usually the F.O.B. invoice amount plus freight plus any special C.O.D. charges. *Note*: This procedure will work only if you use specialized delivery services, such as U.S. Postal Service, United Parcel Service, Federal Express, etc.

Pro Forma: Used for prepayment. You prepare a standard invoice covering all of the costs agreed to (product and freight, for example) and type on the front of the invoice the word: "pro forma." Send the pro-forma invoice to your customer, and ship product on receipt of payment. Pro forma invoices are rarely used for domestic shipments (and then only in circumstances in which credit cannot be established or customer refuses C.O.D.). They are employed generally in those cases where buyer access to funds requires supporting papers, such as certificates of origin, etc.

Guarantees: The only guarantee you will make will be against defects. If damage occurs during shipping, the buyer is usually called upon to pursue a claim with the freight company; however, it will be in your best interest to assist by offering to replace the damaged merchandise. Otherwise, some buyers will withhold payment of your invoice until the freight claim is resolved.

GUIDELINES FOR SUCCESS
Pricing Flow Worksheet

		Competitor's Product	Your Product
1.	Price to consumer	$_____	_____
2.	Less 40% (Retailer profit margin)	x 60%	x 60%
3.	Equals cost to retailer	$_____	_____
4.	Price to retailer (Same as 3)	$_____	_____
5.	Less 25% (Distributor profit margin)	x 75%	x 75%
6.	Equals cost to distributor	$_____	_____
7.	Price to distributor (same as 6)	$_____	_____
8.	Less 20% (Your profit margin)	x 80%	x 80%
9.	Equals exwarehouse cost	$_____	_____

Key question: How do the exwarehouse costs compare?

WAREHOUSING AND SHIPPING THE PRODUCT

Public Warehouses

These are companies that provide storage and warehouse services. Some offer cooled and refrigerated environments. They charge either flat rates by the month, or rates based on product stored, plus in-and-out charges, plus charges for preparing shipping documents (bills of lading), repacking damaged or broken products (coopering), and other related services. If you require public warehousing, then you should shop around to find the best combination of location, services and costs.

Many warehouses will take your orders over the telephone and ship according to your instructions. This is where a facsimile (fax) machine can come in handy.

Storage and warehousing will be an important factor in determining your exwarehouse costs.

Common Carriers

Common carriers are trucking companies, other than the United Parcel Service (UPS), and Parcel Post, which offer pick-up and delivery service. You will have to use common carriers for shipping large orders. UPS will take any size order, but no one container can weigh over 70 pounds (you can save money sometimes by delivering large orders in two or more shipments on UPS). Note that most common carrier charges are based on a minimum shipment rate of 500 pounds.

Your customer may request that you ship via a certain carrier. Most common carriers offer discount rates that are based on total shipment weight. UPS rates are based on the gross weight per case. Gross weight includes the product, outer carton, and shipping materials.

Rates are keyed to hundredweight, or per CWT (cost per hundred pounds). For example, if the quote is $4.00 CWT, then you will pay four cents per pound. Ask your warehouse to find the least expensive and most reliable carrier to fill your requirements.

If your production facility and warehouse are in your home, then you may have trouble working with a common carrier. They will be pleased to pick up and deliver your product, but you will have to arrange for the sometimes difficult process of working without a standard loading dock. Getting the product from your basement, or kitchen, out the front door and onto the truck can be a trial.

Private Pickup and Delivery Services

The United Parcel Service is one of the largest and best known of the pickup and delivery services. Call your local UPS office and request an information kit. They will set up an account for you. They may require you to remit a deposit against which charges for shipping will be made. Generally, they charge a weekly fee for making daily calls at your pickup point. Shipments are charged by the pound, based on destination, and they offer re-delivery, next-day, second-day air, and C.O.D. services.

GUIDELINES FOR SUCCESS
Warehousing and Shipping

Establish Warehouse Arrangements: Shop around for the best deal. A non-union warehouse offers greater leeway to remove samples, take inventory, etc., and is less expensive than union, or "covered," warehouses.

Inbound: Your product is shipped from your production facility, or pier, to the public warehouse.

Stocked: It is inventoried and stocked in the warehouse.

Paperwork/Records: You will receive a monthly inventory statement and invoice for services provided, preparation of bills of lading (the shipping documents), storage, etc.

Select Carrier: You may request the warehouse to select a common carrier to ship your products to your customers. If you have frequent UPS shipments, you can also arrange for United Parcel Service to make daily calls on the warehouse to pick up and deliver the shipments to your customer.

Take inventory: Once a quarter, or more frequently, you should personally supervise a physical inventory in the warehouse. This gives you a good inventory figure to use in preparing your accounts and in controlling your business, and it helps resolve any issues of missing or damaged merchandise.

Guidelines for Success
Warehouse Selection Flow Chart

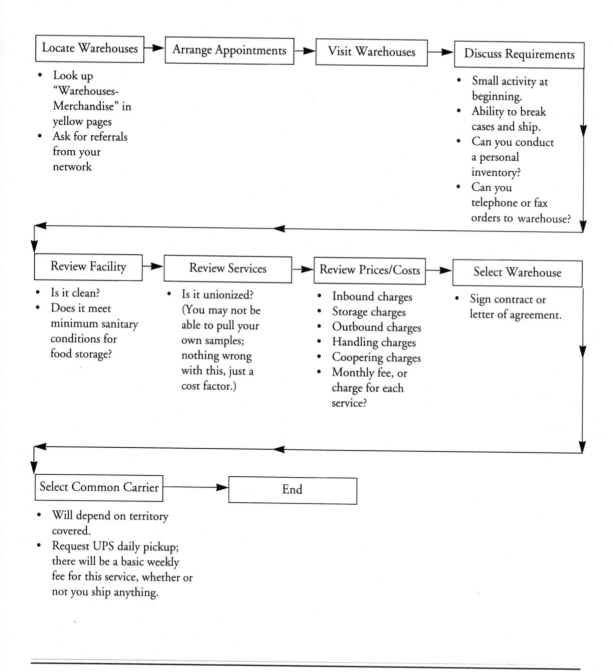

Locate Warehouses → **Arrange Appointments** → **Visit Warehouses** → **Discuss Requirements**

Locate Warehouses
- Look up "Warehouses-Merchandise" in yellow pages
- Ask for referrals from your network

Discuss Requirements
- Small activity at beginning.
- Ability to break cases and ship.
- Can you conduct a personal inventory?
- Can you telephone or fax orders to warehouse?

Review Facility → **Review Services** → **Review Prices/Costs** → **Select Warehouse**

Review Facility
- Is it clean?
- Does it meet minimum sanitary conditions for food storage?

Review Services
- Is it unionized? (You may not be able to pull your own samples; nothing wrong with this, just a cost factor.)

Review Prices/Costs
- Inbound charges
- Storage charges
- Outbound charges
- Handling charges
- Coopering charges
- Monthly fee, or charge for each service?

Select Warehouse
- Sign contract or letter of agreement.

Select Common Carrier → **End**

Select Common Carrier
- Will depend on territory covered.
- Request UPS daily pickup; there will be a basic weekly fee for this service, whether or not you ship anything.

CHAPTER THREE
TAKING YOUR
PRODUCT TO MARKET

This chapter offers a comprehensive review of the most fundamental aspect of specialty food marketing—taking your product to market. The chapter addresses the following elements:

- Preparing Sales Literature
- Designing Point of Purchase Materials
- Promoting the Product
- Advertising the Product
- Finding Buyers
- Establishing Distribution Channels
- Arranging the Deals
- Appointing Brokers
- Locating Distributors
- Making the Sale

You've come a long way in developing your product, and now you want to do a first class job of placing it before the consumer. Your product is tried and tested, packaged and priced. You have identified your niche and are ready to answer why you stayed with the enterprise: to promote, market, sell, and reap your rewards. Before you begin this undertaking, you may want to review the following six principles of marketing that will underlie all your efforts.

1. *Focus*—Ground your business on the consumer, not the distributor or retailer. Know your market and be able to identify your consumer precisely.

2. *Positioning*—Ensure that your product is not at a disadvantage to the competition. Differentiate sufficiently to clinch consumer acceptance.

3. *Demonstrations*—Demos sell. Provide tasting opportunities as often as possible.

4. *Advertising*—Center your advertising on the one specific advantage or edge your product has over the competition. Employ proven advertising methods.

5. *Distribution*—Establish distribution sufficient to the needs of the market. Make sure there is product in distribution to meet consumer demand, especially if you do any consumer advertising.

6. *Promotion*—Manage your promotions to increase in-store display to produce greater consumer sales.

PREPARING SALES LITERATURE

Product sales literature is essential to your sales effort. A sales kit may consist of a price list, catalog (product presentation) sheet, product information sheet, and point of purchase material.

Typically, a catalog sheet and a price sheet will suffice. The catalog sheet is generally an 8-½" by 11" four color, product photograph accompanied

Effective Sales Literature Can Help

❖ Improve distributor and broker knowledge of your product.

❖ Convey preferred use.

❖ Promote the product.

❖ Make sales.

by approximately fifty words of copy that describe the product. Include company name, address, telephone and fax numbers.

In addition to price lists and catalog sheets, you may use a fact sheet to highlight promotable elements of your company and its products. Such elements as testimonials from famous people, historical anecdotes about your company, claims to fame, etc. can be included in the fact sheet. Also, this is where you can amplify statements regarding recipes, applications, and health claims that relate to your product. These provide even more re-enforcement of your sales message. Information that you include on your fact sheets may also be included on your price sheets. Lose no opportunity to impart your sales message!

GUIDELINES FOR SUCCESS
Sales Literature

What to include:

Product description   Make it sizzle! Include the facts and figures (sizes, net contents, case lots, etc.) on the reverse of the catalog sheet. Use the front for the general presentation, and the back for the details.

Photography/graphics   Top notch, upscale.

Copy   Sell the product benefits.

Contact information   Company name, address, telephone number (don't forget area code), and fax.

What not to include:
- Prices
- Dates
- Any "time-sensitive" material (example: "just in time for Valentine's Day 1993").

SELECTING POINT-OF-PURCHASE MATERIALS

Many retailers find point-of-purchase materials (also referred to as P.O.P.) useful in attracting attention to products they stock. P.O.P.'s not only attract consumer attention, they also inform and educate the prospective buyer about the product's benefits. P.O.P.'s may include tent cards (used primarily in restaurants), posters, shelf talkers, product information neck tags attached to bottles and other packages, and recipe handouts.

Tent Cards are small, tent-shaped cards that can be placed on counters, tables and shelves. You have seen these used in restaurants to promote specials of the day, for example. Retailers use them to promote new products and to alert customers about items on sale.

Posters are used in store windows, on store walls, and, when properly mounted, on shelves and counters. Because of their size, many retailers are hesitant to use posters, but they are especially useful during in-store promotions and in trade show exhibits.

Shelf Talkers are used extensively in the grocery trade. They are small signs that are designed to protrude from underneath the product they describe. They can be effective for new product introductions and are more likely to be utilized than posters. Also, they are placed under the product, rather than nearby, making a clear connection between the message they impart and the product they promote.

Product Information tags are most often used in the form of neck tags, which provide all kinds of promotional data. They may include recipes, company history, product uses, recommendations, ingredient descriptions, coupons and free offers. The benefit is that you can insure their use because they require no extra effort on the part of the retailer—they are already affixed to the product.

GUIDELINES FOR SUCCESS
Point-of-Purchase Materials

	Tent cards	**Posters**	**Shelf Talkers**	**Neck Tags**
Size (approx):	5" x 7"	18" x 36"	6" x 10"	2 ¾" x 2 ½"
Color:	2-Color	4-Color	2-Color	2 or 4-Color
Number to Prepare:	1,000	500	1,000	One run's worth
Distribution:	Foodservice/ Retailers	Retailers	Distributors	With the Product
When to use:	Demos/Special Events	New Products/ New Retailers	New Products/ New Retailers	During Intro Stage/ New Products

Notes:

Size:

Tent cards are used on tables, so the size is small and the message brief. I have used posters with cardboard backing that can stand alone or be placed on a wall. In both cases, the posters were 9" x 14". Shelf talker size may be limited by the number of shelf "facings" available for your product. You don't want your shelf talker to use space occupied by another product. Neck tags are small and can be unfolded to reveal several pages of product information.

Color:

2-color products are recommended, where possible, to save money.

Number to prepare:

Go slowly, prepare as few as economically feasible.

Distribution and when to use:

Tent cards, posters, and shelf talkers can be shipped either with the product or via your broker and/or distributor. Neck tags may be used all the time.

PROMOTING THE PRODUCT

One of the most important elements of niche marketing is product promotion. Product promotion often means the difference between success or failure. Getting your product before the consumer and having it recognized is the first step to making a sale. One of the most important promotional vehicles is a trade show. Other promotional vehicles are described later in this section.

Trade Shows

A cost-effective means of introducing a new product, gathering market research, learning about competition, and making sales can be achieved by participation in a food show. There are numerous food shows, but few offer real value to most specialty food producers. See Appendix A for a listing of some of the prominent food shows.

The major shows held in the United States attract buyers from most specialty food markets. The level of exposure at these shows can be met or improved on only by undertaking the time and cost of traveling to many of the leading specialty food markets.

Certain trade shows require exhibitors to be members of the sponsoring association. Some associations require you to be in business for at least two years in order to be accepted as a member. If a member distributor or broker takes on your product, and thereby develops a client business relationship with you, then your products can be exhibited in that distributor's or broker's booth.

The estimated current cost for a 100 square foot booth, with minimum spot lighting, drayage, table covers, freight in and out, travel, accommodations and meals for one person is approximately $4,000.00.

Before attending a trade show, you will have to consider the appropriateness of your sales literature for the target market including the illustration and

Benefits of Food Show Participation

- ❖ Meet customers.

- ❖ Learn about competition.

- ❖ Experiment with product ingredients.

- ❖ Evaluate product packaging.

- ❖ Test product pricing.

- ❖ Rate various promotion techniques.

- ❖ Identify important trends.

- ❖ Solicit customer reaction.

- ❖ Make sales.

currency of information. You will have to consider booth design, layout, signs, demo equipment requirements (you will have to order display risers, electricity, and floodlighting). Standard booth order generally includes tables, chairs, and booth carpeting.

Negotiations with potential distributors:

- Pricing/deals
- Length of contract
- Post-sales support/Training
- Performance measurements
- Territory
- Promotional activities—who pays?

As promotional tools, trade shows should be a part of a fully integrated and well-managed campaign. Trade shows should be incorporated into other promotional efforts for full effect.

GUIDELINES FOR SUCCESS
Trade Show Milestones

One year before show

- ☐ Commit to attending the trade show.
- ☐ Begin work on total promotion campaign.
- ☐ Review booth design. Look for imaginative, inexpensive display schemes/materials.

Six months before show

- ☐ Make plane reservations and hotel accommodations.
- ☐ Develop sales literature for show.

Three months before show

- ☐ Check on sales literature produced by both your firm and the show sponsor.
- ☐ Review results in search for prospective brokers and distributors.
- ☐ Initiate contact and establish appointments with key prospects.

Two months before show

- ☐ Arrange shipment of any display equipment and samples (all display materials must be fireproofed).
- ☐ Prepare press kits.
- ☐ Verify with freight forwarder that equipment has arrived. (Note: You can hand-carry samples/display materials from your car to the show booth. Generally, you cannot use any luggage carts or trolleys.)
- ☐ Confirm with show management that all arrangements have been made regarding shipping, electricity, extra tables/chairs, table drapes, signs, etc.
- ☐ Determine method for lead qualification following the show.
- ☐ Hand-carry "just-in-case" package of samples, price sheets, literature.

Upon arrival

- ☐ Set up booth display (table covers, samples, signs, etc.).
- ☐ Become familiar with show layout, transportation, special events, etc.
- ☐ Deliver your press kits to the show Press Room.
- ☐ Survey competitors' products, booths, product literature.

Upon returning home

- ☐ Write thank you notes to the appropriate people.
- ☐ Record recommendations for successive shows.
- ☐ Begin business follow-up with potential customers.

GUIDELINES FOR SUCCESS
How to Reduce Trade Show Expenses

1. Share booth with another food producer.
2. Share booth with broker/distributor.
3. Take your own (flameproof) table drapes and riser covers. (Use a colorful oilcloth-type table cover for easy cleaning.)
4. Use your own posters and signs.
5. Order one double-neck floodlight per 100 square feet of exhibit space.
6. Hand-carry your samples (no luggage carts with freight permitted through show doors, but you can carry boxes).
7. Bring a Dustbuster to clean your carpet (touch up).
8. Survival gear:

   _____ Packaging tape/dispenser   _____ Fishing line (to hang posters)
   _____ Cellophane tape   _____ Paper napkins   _____ Marking pens
   _____ Pliers   _____ Stapler/staples   _____ Ballpoint pens
   _____ Clipboard   _____ Screw driver   _____ Business cards

9. Take a styrofoam cooler (for samples, cold drinks, snacks, etc.).
10. Use ice from outside exhibit hall for your cooler.
11. Take hot plate (if required for sample tasting).
12. Take serving materials (plastic plates, bowls, spoons, forks, etc.).
13. Consider a less expensive hotel, and commute to the show.

Aside from the all-important trade shows, specialty food promotion can take many forms, some of the most common are described below.

In-Store Demonstrations/Tastings

Consumers tend to buy products they have sampled, usually at sample tastings conducted at the point of purchase. These can involve a demonstrator, your product, and the means of sampling (crackers with cheese, for example). The demonstration is conducted during high traffic periods, over the course of three to six hours. Consumers have the opportunity to taste your product, to comment on it, to hear a pitch from the demonstrator, and to purchase. Often, demonstrations are accompanied by a special product price used to entice the consumer into making an immediate purchase.

A typical demonstration might be conducted from 10:00A.M. to 3:00P.M. on a Saturday. The idea is to get as much public attention as you can, so peak shopping hours are best for demonstrations. Demonstrator costs will be in the neighborhood of $10.00 to $20.00 per hour, with a $75.00 to $100.00 minimum fee per day.

Giveaways

One of the least expensive forms of advertising and promotion is a product giveaway. A carefully managed program of free merchandise can place your product in front of the consumer, while attracting the attention of the retailer.

Usually, free merchandise is offered with in-store demonstrations, introductory deals, and sampling allowances. Free merchandise may also include specially packed sample containers for distribution at the point of purchase and during trade shows.

Mailings

A mailing can consist of a price list, a sample, and a catalog sheet sent to several retailers and/or distributors, or it can consist of a mass mailing with multiple inserts, full color slick catalog sheets, and samples to thousands of prospective consumers. In entry-level niche marketing, mailings will be limited more than likely to selected retailers and distributors.

It is very difficult for a new supplier to sell a new and unseen food product via the mail.

Mailings should be made to prospective distributors in accordance with a complete marketing promotion. In other words, generate more than just a mailing! Devise a follow-up program that will include telephone screening and sales calls. *A mailing should sell as well as inform.*

Case In Point

General Foods Corporation, with all its resources, was unable to make a success out of its much ballyhooed Thomas Garroway, Ltd. mail-order speciality foods division. The company spent millions of dollars on full page, four-color, advertising in major consumer magazines in an effort to sell gourmet foods by mail. I know of no successful gourmet foods by mail enterprise in which a company ships a variety of different foods direct to consumers.

Case In Point

The following is an example of possible overkill in a mailing to retailers.

The following materials were received in an 8-¾" by 6" envelope sent via bulk mail to retailers in January 1992 by a two-year old specialty food company that specializes in distinctive baked goods and confectionery:

- *2 empty cookie boxes, each with one-cookie capacity (0.75 oz).*
- *1 "deal" sheet describing two deals.*
- *1 empty cheesecake box (to hold one miniature 0.4 oz cheesecake).*
- *1 empty 1.5 oz cookie box, to hold two cookies.*
- *1 mailing list inquiry return card, with special offer.*
- *1 "valuable coupon" to save $10.00 off the regular price of a national retailer directory.*
- *1 corporate logo private label offer and sample cookie box (for your logo, their cookie, and a cookie carton company's cookie carton).*
- *1 six-page, four-color, 8-½" x 11" brochure that includes a price list and order form.*

Note: This is a very expensive, major mailing. Such direct mailings, in which "more is more" are atypical in the specialty food trade, simply because they cost so much to conduct.

Mailings to retailers are slightly different than mailings to distributors. Usually, they do not include the follow-up telephone call or the sales call. You will be mailing to many retailers, instead of a couple of dozen distributors, so you design a different mail campaign. The inserts you use should include a postage paid return order form for easy use by the retailer. Mailings to retailers are best used as: information providers, invitations to visit your trade show booth, invitations to request free samples or more information and inducements to re-order.

GUIDELINES FOR SUCCESS
Mailings to Distributors

1. Develop a mailing list. (May be purchased through a mailing list broker. See listing in Appendices.)

2. Prepare the mailer. Include a cover letter, catalog/price sheet, and a sample (if possible). Cover letter should be brief, informative, and to the point. State that you will telephone the buyer "next week."

3. Prepare the envelope.

4. Mail the materials.

5. Follow-up by telephone in about seven days.

6. Qualify the buyer (discern level of interest).

7. Arrange an appointment.

8. Send a brief note confirming appointment details, and stressing a benefit of your product.

9. Call on the prospect, stress the benefits, and make the sale!

10. Follow-up with a brief note about sale details.

Tie-Ins

You can get more out of your promotion dollar by sharing the costs with another food producer. This is accomplished by "tying" your product with another complementary product, for example, tea with pastries/cakes/cookies; cheese with crackers; preserves with special muffins/breads.

Arrange to have a series of in-store demonstrations conducted where both products are being served. Share the costs of the demonstration with the other producer. The tie-in concept can be supported by presenting the two products in a special promotional package.

Testimonials and Show Awards

One of the most effective, and least expensive, promotional tools is to get someone who is in the public eye to say something nice about your product. Send your samples and product information to all of the important food editors in your major markets; as well as food preparing personalities who appear on radio and television. Include a press kit with press release, sample (if possible), company history/data, and a listing of where the product can be purchased. To assist you, if your budget permits, you may wish to have this accomplished by a professional public relations firm.

Submit your product to trade show managements that have product award committees. Your product will be evaluated against many others, but if you win "best new product for such-and-such year," you can use this in your product literature, trade show exhibits, and advertisements. Both the testimonials and show awards offer third party endorsements that attest to the quality of your product.

GUIDELINES FOR SUCCESS
Promotion Examples
From the *Gourmet News* magazine, United Publications, Inc., P.O. Box 1056, Yarmouth, ME 04096

Company	Product	Promotion	Dates	Region
Ducktrap River Fish Farm	Trout fillet	Reduced price during Lent, recipe cards or promotional material provided.	4 Mar-12 Apr	Nat'l
Festive Foods	Buffalo Bob's Bodacious BBQ Bracer	15% discount.	Mar-Apr	Nat'l
Fox Hollow Farm	Fox More Than a Mustard	Sale pricing plus 1 oz. bonus in each jar.	Mar-Aug	Nat'l
Gilbey's Int'l	Mrs. Beaton's Foods	15% discount.	March	Nat'l
John Wagner & Sons	Honey-sweetened preserves, Country Cupboard salad dressings	15% discount.	Mar-Apr	Nat'l
Perugina Chocolate	Classic Bars	8% off invoice allowance.	Mar-Jun	Nat'l
Peachtree Specialties	Syrups, sauces, and dressings	15% off plus free in-store samples when you tell us you read about it in *Gourmet News*.	March	Nat'l
Fowler's Milling Company	Pancake, muffin, cookie mixes	Display cartons with point of purchase info.	Mar-Jun	Nat'l
Mendocino Pasta	Fresh-dried flavored fettucini	New pasta for pasta storage rack, including recipe booklet.	Through Dec.	No. CA

ADVERTISING THE PRODUCT

We tend to think that consumer advertising is the easy way to draw attention to our product. In the first place, your product has to be in the market before an advertisement directed at the consumer will work.

Occasionally, consumers will see inserts in the likes of *Gourmet, The New Yorker, Smithsonian,* and other magazines that advertise fancy foods; however, in the specialty food industry, the only advertisements that seem to be directed to consumers with any regularity in those magazines are ones that offer product via mail order instead of through retail stores. Successful consumer advertising requires ingenuity and deep pockets. According to the American Association of Advertising Agencies, the average American is exposed to approximately 7,000 advertising stimuli a day.

You are well advised to tread lightly when it comes to consumer advertising, especially if you are considering television or radio. Stick with advertising inserts in specialty food trade journals. See Appendix B for a listing of trade journals devoted to this industry.

Media Selection

Several of the trade journals will work with you to save money in preparing your advertisement. Consider retaining a small and hungry advertising agency. It will cost a little more, but the result will be better than cutting and pasting on your own. Make sure that advertising costs are figured into your overall budget in an amount equal to ten to fifteen percent of sales, or projected sales.

Some advertising can be accomplished using local radio and newspapers, but this is best done in connection with larger retailer promotions, such as those conducted by department stores.

What you undertake in the form of advertising will be determined by available funds. You will depend more on your own resources if you have a $1,000 budget and more on outside help if you have a $10,000 budget.

Advertising Costs

Insert preparation—($2,000 to $3,000): An insert is the actual advertisement you will have "inserted" in the magazine/newspaper. Many specialty food trade journals will take your camera-ready art work and produce it as an advertisement. You can expect to pay upwards of $3,000 for a black and white ad with about fifty words of copy. Illustrations and photography will cost extra. Cost factors in a one-half page black and white insert include: art work, mechanical preparation, copywriting and typesetting.

Photography—($400 to $1,000): If you have a photograph made of your product, or product line, then arrange to use the same photograph in your catalog sheets and other promotional materials.

Typical costs of insert space—($1,200 to $3,300 and up): Media costs (the magazine or newspaper space) to insert 1/2 page (vertical or horizontal) black and white ad, for example, will range from $1,200 to $1,800, depending on the magazine/newspaper. These costs can be discounted by running the ad more than once.

GUIDELINES FOR SUCCESS
Advertising Hints

❖ Use the advertisement over the course of twelve months, or longer, and in a number of issues of different trade journals.

❖ Make certain the art work and mechanical designed for the advertisement can be used in point-of-purchase posters and other promotional materials.

❖ Use the advertisement in combination with a well-planned and effectively managed advertising and promotion program.

❖ Coordinate advertising inserts with press releases, in-store promotions, show displays, mailings, and point-of-purchase posters.

❖ Don't waste money by running one fancy advertisement only once or twice in a single journal.

❖ Coordinate promotions with current and prospective retailer and distributor promotions.

FINDING BUYERS

Now that you have had your product produced, packaged, and labeled, how do you find the specific buyers identified as a category during your initial market research? The type of customer you identify will depend on the type of product you have to sell. Whether the product is canned, fresh, frozen, or refrigerated will influence its distribution possibilities.

Identifying the Potential Customer

We have numbered approximately 23,000 retailer prospects as potential buyers of your product. This figure presumes a product not requiring special handling and display, such as frozen and refrigerated foods. It presumes also an ability to get the product to all these prospects. About 15,000 of them will be able to stock refrigerated items such as cheese and fresh pâté. The competition for that space will be keen.

The number of retailer prospects swells substantially if your product can be sold in a gift store, of which there are approximately 71,000! Our 23,000 retailer figure includes only ten percent of these as devoting any shelf space to specialty foods. More often than not, a gift store will carry a food product, notably candy, and will merchandise it as a gift, rather than food.

There are approximately five dozen distributors that specialize in selling specialty food to retailers. In addition, full-line grocery distributors, of which there are hundreds, are carrying more specialty foods every year.

Qualifying Potential Buyers

Qualifying a buyer involves assessing the potential interest and likelihood of making a purchase. In the case of distributors, you do this by reviewing the product lines currently carried, mailing information, sending samples, and following up by telephone. Once you have qualified your buyer, you can then make arrangements to set an appointment for a sales call.

You can rely on your broker to qualify retailers, or you can make the call yourself to determine the interest level and to make the sale.

Guidelines for Success
Hints for Finding Buyers

❖ Exhibit in major (national and regional) specialty food trade shows.

❖ Arrange for one of the specialty food trade journals to conduct a mailing on your behalf.

❖ Contact the N.A.S.F.T. for information about their retailer and distributor members.

❖ Purchase a mailing list of gourmet food retailers from available business list consolidation services (Appendix L).

❖ Contact National Specialty Food Distributor Association for member list (Appendix E).

❖ Contact National Specialty Food Brokers Association for member list, brokers can help you find buyers. (See Appendix D.)

Establishing Distribution Channels

You will employ various channels of distribution to get your product to the consumer. Understanding these distribution options will enable you to refine your marketing plans. In the specialty food trade, you will use either distributors (also called store-door distributors, full service distributors, jobbers, and wholesalers), retailers (including gourmet food stores, warehouse clubs, department stores and mass merchandisers), direct mail, and/or catalog houses.

The exact type of distribution used will depend on a number of factors, some of which include:

◆ the market segment (by product type, geographic region, etc.)
◆ the expected sales volume (large volume may require different distribution capabilities)
◆ the nature of the product promotion.

The profusion of specialty foods has made the process of obtaining distributor interest in carrying new products increasingly difficult. As a result, distribution often will require that you do all the pioneering yourself (selling direct to retailers) in order to attract the attention of a distributor. If you are lucky, your product may have sufficient appeal to attract a distributor as soon as you introduce it.

Before you approach a distributor, you should review certain aspects of the specialty foods business. This list includes the topics you should know and which are contained in this book. Consult the contents or index for page numbers.

- ◆ How specialty foods get to the consumer.
- ◆ The role of the distributor in this process.
- ◆ Required profit margin/promotion support.
- ◆ The relevance of introductory deals.
- ◆ Details of your competition.
- ◆ Specialty food pricing strategies.
- ◆ Specialty food promotion strategies.
- ◆ Marketing elements specific to the territory.

How Distribution Works

Distribution depends on the product, season, market segment, region, product stage of development, and consumer awareness/perception/attitudes. As mentioned in the introduction to this guide, as soon as you find a profitable way to distribute your product, someone else will be doing just as well with a similar product, but with an entirely different distribution strategy. There are a number of distribution avenues open to you.

You can sell direct to the consumer by running your own retail operation, either in a permanent setting, or at special holiday fairs, for example. You can also do this via mail order. Make a mailing to prospective customers or take out a mail order advertisement.

You can reach the consumer via a retailer which will probably be your initial means of entering the specialty food industry. You put the samples in the trunk of your car and call on as many retailers as

Distributor Options Vary by Annual Sales Volume

Your distribution options will be more sophisticated at higher levels of gross revenues. Also, higher revenues will mean a greater commitment to funding advertising and promotion programs. The following describes the approximate distinctions between varying levels of sales and distribution schemes.

High volume sales (+$1 million): Buyer has own warehouse—mass merchandising—significant advertising dollars required. Not a major factor in specialty food distribution.

For medium volume sales ($500,000 to $1 million): To supermarkets via rack jobbers (they do all the shelf work). Costs can include demos and free merchandise. Some specialty food distributors have established relationships with both independent and major supermarket chains.

For low volume sales (generally under $500,000): To store backdoor via wholesaler/distributor who uses brokers and own sales force or direct to store via your broker. This is the primary distribution option used in specialty food trade.

possible to make sales. Or make the sale and then ship to the customer via UPS.

Selling through a broker to a retailer is similar to the above, but instead of doing it yourself, a commissioned broker takes your samples to the retailers in his or her territory and makes the sales calls.

You may also reach your market through a distributor to a retailer. The distributor buys your product and sells it to the retailer. Some products, especially heavy products in jars, generally require distribution in this manner. It tends to be too expensive to design the containers required to ship a dozen jars via UPS so they arrive undamaged at the retailer's door. (Nevertheless, direct to retailer sales are often necessary for the beginner, in order to create interest from the distributor.)

Sales are also made via a broker to a distributor to a retailer. Again, you employ a commissioned broker to take your samples and to make sales calls on distributors.

Your product may be sold via a catalog house, although very few catalogs have been successful selling retail packaged specialty foods. Those that are successful usually sell products that can be used as gifts. Some catalog companies will ask you to "drop ship." This means that they send you the order and a mailing label, and you ship the individual product directly to the consumer. You are paid by the catalog company. You may also use a broker to make sales to a catalog house.

Significance of Exclusivity

All brokers and many distributors will ask for an exclusive territory. With brokers, the exclusive arrangement is to your advantage. It makes little sense to have two brokers competing for the same buyer with the same products.

Distributors often request exclusivity, especially when introducing a new product. It will make some sense to work closely with a distributor in a given market on an exclusive basis. This helps rationalize your marketing and distribution strategy. You might want to limit the arrangement, depending on the distributor and on the market, to six months.

Some strategies work for some producers and not for others. Many successful specialty food producers have never offered any exclusive arrangements. Once again, it depends on the timing, territory, product, price, etc. One way to ascertain distributor interest in an exclusive arrangement is to ask what sort of volume is guaranteed?

Food Service

A growing segment of the specialty food trade consists of selling to hotels, restaurants, and institutions—better food service. Distribution in this market segment requires the use of brokers and distributors who sell to food service accounts. Food service opportunities exist for specialty food producers who supply fancy jams, preserves and syrups and the like in single servings for use on hotel restaurant tables, in room service and other situations such as take out orders and picnic baskets.

Offering single-serving food products to food service outlets adds an opportunity to attain sampling and brand awareness because single serving packages will be labeled with your brand name.

Providing your product for use as a *prepared food ingredient* will meet increasing demand by restaurants that are preparing more foods with specialty food ingredients. It is also a way to generate revenue during your start-up stage, and to reduce product costs by arranging for larger production runs. On the other hand, there is little "branding" opportunity for your products sold in institutional containers, and you will be subject to the vagaries of food service trends.

Specialty Food Distribution Channels with Incremental Profit Margins/Commissions

Producer ....Via Distributor ....To Retailer
                                         (30%)   (40%)

Producer..Via Broker ....To Retailer
                                 (10% commission)   (40%)

Producer......................Via Broker ....Via Distributor ....To Retailer
                (5% commission)   (30%)   (40%)

Producer ....Via Broker ....Via Distributor............Via Broker ....To Retailer
     (5% commission)   (30%)   (*)   (40%)

Producer ....To Retailer
                                                                                             (40%)

* Commission paid from distributor's share of profit margin.

The food service sector is extremely price conscious. High priced products are better served by creating demand first at retail, instead of wasting too much time exploring the food service segment. The market is there, but you must be price competitive to crack it.

ARRANGING THE DEALS

Because of the risk involved, both in terms of wasted time and expended resources, few of your potential customers will be willing to carry a new product automatically. Consequently, most retailers, and particularly distributors, require special deals in order to earn extra profit during start-up and to introduce your product successfully.

The most common is the "introductory" deal. This can involve some combination of those described below. With all deals, you can offer a "sixty-day buy-in" that allows the buyer to purchase up to a pre-determined credit limit for sixty days and get the introductory deal.

Competition is so stiff in this industry that getting retailers and distributors to even try your product can be a major undertaking. The reasoning behind the deals is to help the buyer justify some of the costs and risks associated with introducing, or pioneering, the product. Most distributors, for example, would like to be assured of their normal profit at the outset of a product introduction, in the event the product does not succeed. In this way, they do not suffer a loss. They do not have to wait until the product takes off before they make a profit. The cost of deals is a cost to you, just as are ingredients, and must be budgeted and controlled accordingly.

Competition is so stiff in this industry that getting retailers and distributors to even try your product can be a major undertaking.

Deals offer extra profits to the buyer, lower selling prices to attract customers, sources of funding for advertising/promotion and assistance in gaining attention over competing brands.

Note: Many of the following deals/allowances should be offered only if asked for by the buyer, and considered only if you feel the overall benefit is worth the expense. Weigh your decision carefully. You will want to develop a long term relationship with the buyer that may not evolve if at first you give the product away, and then later withdraw the deal.

Free Merchandise

"One free case with ten, the 11th case is free." The distributors or retailers may use the free product in any way they wish. The retailers may choose to pass the savings along to the consumer, or the distributors may pass it along to the retailer, or either may take the difference to defer the cost of introducing the product and to increase profits. Note that this differs from the offer "one free case in ten." One *with* is preferred because you ship more product, which is, after all, the point. One free case with ten amounts to a 9.1% discount.

If you specify that the free goods are for the retailer, then obtain proof of delivery for free merchandise shipped from the distributor to the retailer. In this way, you have greater assurance that your product gets to the customer, and you get the names and addresses of the customers.

Sampling Allowance

Another free merchandise offer involves providing free product to the distributor (or retailer) so that free samples can be offered to consumers. This can also help the distributor get a retailer to purchase for the first time.

Demonstration Allowance

The "demo allowance" can combine free product along with a cash discount to cover the cost of a demonstrator. The demonstrator is retained either by you, the retailer, or the distributor, to serve and promote your product in the retail store. Ascertain beforehand the demonstrator's abilities, and the day and time for the intended demonstration. If possible, control and monitor the demonstration carefully, for experience shows that the absence of active producer involvement in control of demonstrations can waste time and money.

Prepare a standard demonstration kit that contains procedures you want to be followed in order for the demonstrator to be paid. It should include detailed instructions and an evaluation form that must be sent to you after the completed demonstration.

Demonstration costs vary, depending on the store and on the nature and length of the demonstration. Please refer to the section on promotion earlier in this chapter for a discussion of demonstration costs.

Special Terms

Many companies offer a discount for payment within ten days. This can be expressed as 2%, 10 days, NET 30 days, F.O.B warehouse. This means

Here are some other free merchandise discount percentages:

1 free with 2	=	33.3%
1 free with 3	=	25.0%
1 free with 5	=	16.7%
1 free with 12	=	7.7%
1 free with 20	=	4.7%
1 free with 25	=	3.8%

that the distributor and retailer will pay the freight (either freight collect, or added to the invoice), and that their payment must be received by you on the 10th day, with a 2% discount, or in the full amount by the 30th day after delivery.

As an introductory deal, you can offer special terms to the distributor, such as: 2%, 30 days, delivered, which means that you pay the freight, and the buyer takes a deduction of 2% from the F.O.B. invoice amount, which is due in 30 days.

You can offer any combination of these to either the distributor, or to the retailer. My recommendation is to stick to your original terms, unless it is a major purchase that would not work without special terms.

Freight Allowance

You can peg these to volume orders. For example, you might offer a five percent freight allowance for any order over fifty cases of assorted product. This means that the buyer may deduct five percent of the F.O.B. invoice amount from the payment. The idea is to encourage larger purchases by offering the benefit of economy to the buyer.

You can also calculate freight into your prices. Link these with three geographic zones—East, Central, and West—so that you will have three different, delivered, prices depending on customer location.

Your terms of F.O.B. warehouse mean that the buyer is responsible for the freight costs from your loading dock to his warehouse or store. When selling to distributors, you may have occasion to ship freight collect. This means that the trucking company will pick up and deliver your merchandise and will collect for the freight costs on delivery.

When shipping to a retailer, you may add the freight costs (usually United Parcel Service) to your invoice. Further discussion of shipping procedures and theory appears under Warehousing and Shipping earlier in this chapter.

Slotting Allowance

Some supermarket chains and specialty food distributors will require that you pay them a slotting allowance (also called "push money"). This is a dollar amount, that may be paid in the form of cash or free merchandise, to cover the cost of "slotting" the product in the distributor's warehouse.

Ostensibly, the slotting allowance is exacted from the distributor by the supermarket chain in order to justify the costs, and risks, of taking on a new product. The result is that many new specialty food producers have had to seek other means of distribution, such as direct sales to small retailers, and thereby experience considerable difficulty in establishing full distribution.

If you agree to a slotting fee, then you should demand proof from the distributor that the product has actually reached the store shelves. The requirement for slotting allowances is a fairly recent, hotly debated, and not a universally popular phenomenon.

Advertising and Catalog Allowances

Advertising allowances should be agreed to in advance, with specific elements of proof requested. Such proof of performance can include copies of the advertising inserts or circulars.

Another form of advertising allowance is cooperative advertising, wherein you and the buyer agree to share the cost of an advertisement in a local newspaper, or on a local radio station. You may be requested to provide copy, and black and white slicks (camera-ready art work on glossy stock) that depict your product and/or logo.

Case In Point

A new hitch in the food industry is the so-called "success fee." When a producer introduces a new product, both the producer and the distributor agree to establish sales goals over a defined period. When the goal is achieved, the producer pays the distributor a success fee. Some industry participants have predicted that the success fee will replace the slotting fee over the next five years.

The use of advertising allowances (the buyer deducts the allowance from the invoice) and bill backs (you request the buyer to remit a bill to you at the end of the period) should be restricted to those opportunities that offer the best potential for sales.

Using catalog "houses" is a good way of promoting your product. In order to defray some of the cost of producing a catalog, an allowance, usually ten percent, is required by the catalog companies that will carry your product. This is a promotional cost to you because the catalogs generally carry your product only once, but you do get the residual benefit of putting your product before a large audience.

GUIDELINES FOR SUCCESS
Deals in Review

❖ Free Merchandise - A broadly employed, and cost-effective, means of getting new business.

❖ Sampling Allowance - Similar to Free Merchandise.

❖ Demonstration Allowance - A useful promotional tool. Requires effective management.

❖ Special Terms - Not encouraged. Use only if in special circumstances (*e.g.*, the buyer is planning a major promotion and requests extended payment period).

❖ Freight Allowance - Used to encourage the larger order.

❖ "Free" Freight - Use as special arrangement (trade shows, seasonal specials, etc.).

❖ Slotting Allowance - Mostly required by supermarket chains and larger distributors. Try to avoid.

❖ Advertising Allowance - Use for special promotions (ethnic foods, for example). Monitor carefully.

❖ Catalog Allowance - For catalog sales.

APPOINTING BROKERS

Brokers are manufacturers' representatives. They do not buy your products. They take your product literature, samples and pricing information, and make sales for you in a given territory. Brokers receive a commission for sales made, based on your F.O.B. invoice value. They generally receive ten percent commission for sales to retailers, and five percent commission for sales to distributors. These arrangements, and commissions, can differ depending on the product and the market.

Brokers obtain supermarket authorizations and monitor distributor activity on behalf of the principal. Often referred to as "food reps," food brokers also sell to individual retail accounts, small boutiques, specialty food shops, and gift shops. As food reps, they often maintain a showroom.

Note that most experienced brokers already have extensive lines to represent. On the one hand, a broker with several lines may not be able to devote much attention to your line, while, on the other hand, a new broker may not be able to make a living just selling your product alone. Nevertheless, the system works, and most brokers are interested in exploring new opportunities.

Brokers can exercise an important influence on developing sales for your products. They have access to buyers, knowledge of territories, and experience that you probably could not afford to replace in the form of a full-time sales staff. Brokers carry a number of lines, and they often provide the only cost effective way for you to get your product to stores in regions away from home base.

Because of this, there is a trade-off. Depending on the situation, you may have to take second place in a product lineup carried by a broker who is interested in your product. Unless the broker can see potential for high volume (read "high commission income"), then it will be unlikely for the broker to devote much attention to pioneering your product.

Brokers can help implement your promotion plans, including in-store demonstrations, and new product introductions. You will not require a broker if you can manage the territory yourself.

Locating Brokers

Broker listings are available from the National Association of Specialty Food Brokers (see Appendix D), and from advertisements in various specialty food industry journals (Appendix B). In addition, brokers regularly present themselves for consideration at the fancy food shows.

Broker Management Hints

❖ Visit the broker and make joint calls on key customers *at least* twice a year.

❖ Send monthly, or bimonthly, product information notes.

❖ Inform your broker of new products, testimonials, and all success stories.

❖ Work with the broker on planning your product promotions.

❖ Ask the brokers to visit and work your booths in the major trade shows.

I do not recommend advertising for a broker in trade journals. It is more effective to ask other producers, retailers, and distributors for recommendations and leads, than to take a "shotgun" approach through an industry trade journal. Make certain the prospective broker understands your product, and knows how to sell it. You should meet with the broker to achieve a sense of how effectively you can do business together.

Managing Brokers

Once you have selected a broker, you will prepare a contractual agreement (Appendix P) that stipulates the territory to be covered, conditions of sales, terms, commissions, payment procedures, etc. Remember, brokers work for you in specific, designated territories.

Send the broker a supply of samples, catalog sheets, price sheets, press kits, and other descriptive literature in the quantity requested by the broker. To some extent, you may rely on your broker to provide information regarding the credit history of new accounts. You should also be able to rely on the broker to make a personal attempt to collect any overdue invoices. (Make sure the broker is amenable to this before you retain her/his services.)

Essentially, brokers are your representatives in the field. Treat them well, pay your commissions on time and keep them informed. You will attain a span of attention to your product directly proportional to the amount of time and effort you expend on maintaining the broker's interest. Make it easy for them to make money, and you too, will be rewarded.

Generally, brokers are paid monthly, or after the customer invoice has been paid. This is something you will negotiate when the broker is appointed.

GUIDELINES FOR SUCCESS
Broker Evaluation

☐ Years in business - A well-established broker may not have room for your line.

☐ Territories covered - Is it adequate to your needs?

☐ Major accounts called upon - Do they include your prime targets?

☐ Account requirements for deals, etc. - Can you accommodate these?

☐ Lines currently represented - Do any compete with yours?

☐ Number of sales staff - Sufficient to meet your needs?

☐ References - Contact three of them for comments.

☐ "Success stories" - Especially with lines similar to yours.

LOCATING DISTRIBUTORS

Specialty food distributors (direct store distributors) buy your product for their own account and sell it to retailers, and to other distributors, using their own sales force and independent brokers.

Generally, they offer the specialty food producer a higher volume and profit generating alternative to direct retailer sales. The grocery food distribution system is very efficient. Because of this, it leaves little room for the lower volume specialty food product. Specialty food distributors fill this niche by carrying products that have not yet reached the level of consumption experienced by products in the grocery trade.

Many newer specialty food processors begin by selling direct to the retailer. A number of them retain this method of distributing their products even after they have gained a foothold in the market. With the increasing incidence of slotting allowances (see

Arranging the Deals, earlier in this chapter) most small companies will be unable to afford the cost of introducing a new product through distributors.

Distributors will let you know what they require. To attract their attention, you will most likely have to develop some of their territory first. This means selling direct to retailers. You will have to assess your circumstances carefully, and be prepared for the long haul, if you wish to continue selling direct to the retailer.

Distributor Services

Specialty food distributors offer a variety of services to the producer and to the retailer. Among those services offered by many, but not all, specialty food distributors do the following:

- Make sales calls on retailers and chain buyers.
- Purchase, inventory, and deliver your product to the retailer.
- Stock retailer shelves (usually only at chains).
- Oversee in-store demos.
- Prepare shelf diagrams for optimal display of the product (usually done only at chains).
- Provide product sales and profit data to the retailer.
- Distribute P. O. P. materials (obtained from you).
- Instruct store personnel in benefits of your product.
- Rotate shelf stock and remove unsalable merchandise (usually done only at chains).

Case In Point

Campbell World Trading Company, a division of Campbell Soup Company. Established to market mostly Campbell-owned specialty products in the United States Lines included Lazzaroni, Delacre, and Kambly confections. Sales reportedly approached the $2 million mark. Division disbanded in 1991. Its specialty nature did not fit into the corporate culture at Campbell. Products are now marketed by independent agents and distributors.

GUIDELINES FOR SUCCESS
Appointing Distributors

Consider the following elements before you appoint a distributor:

1. Length of appointment - Your letter of appointment should stipulate the period covered. Example: One year from signing, renewable annually thereafter.

2. Territory covered - Stipulate which state, region or large metropolitan area you are assigning to the distributor.

3. Promotional Support - Determine which combination of advertising allowances, special deals, free merchandise, etc. will be required by the distributor. Negotiate the details that are best suited to your mutual requirements and circumstances.

4. Frequency of contact - You should attempt to be in regular contact with all your distributors. Use mail, telephone, and fax, plus personal visits and combined sales calls.

5. Termination provisions - Your appointment letter should provide the means for terminating the contract. This can be effected in writing by either party with 30 or 60 days advance notice.

Note. In many instances, you may have to take what is available and proceed without any formal appointment. If a distributor wants to buy your product, you cannot refuse on the basis of other distributor arrangements. This can be considered restraint of trade and is against the law; however, you can always appoint your distributor in a given territory as "master distributor." That distributor would then sell to other distributors. In fact, once the distributor buys your product, you have no legal control over what he/she decides to do with it!

MAKING THE SALE

Now that you have an appointment, remember to take product samples, price lists, catalog sheets, pens, and a hand-held calculator. You will need the latter to verify your mental gymnastics. These will come about as you respond to fast questions about various discounts and quantity orders and other details from the buyer.

Use your price list as an order form. This will make it easier to process the order when you return to the office. Generally, you will not be required to give a copy of the order to the buyer. Many distributors will provide you with their own computer-generated order form.

Closing the Sale

The single greatest obstacle to closing a sale, aside from ignorance, is the fear of rejection! We all want friendly environments. We all want everybody to love our product, but we tend to avoid asking the most important question: "Can we write an order?" or "How many cases may I ship you?".

A great salesperson goes for the jugular! He or she never cries "uncle," no matter how many rejections, insults, or refusals received. The process is constantly being improved. No salesperson rests on laurels. All salespeople love selling. Learn about the importance of stressing benefits to the buyers instead of simply pointing out product features. Listen to the buyer and learn how to handle objections (most of which can be turned to your advantage, once you know what to say).

Do not impugn your competition, especially if the competing product is currently carried by the company you are trying to sell to. This puts the buyer in an awkward position, for he/she probably made the decision to carry the other product, and putting the buyer's judgment in question may impede your further progress.

Your first goal has been achieved. You are in the company of a qualified buyer who has expressed an interest in hearing your pitch. Don't lose sight of your objective. It's not to make friends, or to have an informal chat. Your sole objective is to make that sale!

Keep in focus! So many of us go off on tangents. When you are stressing the benefits of purchasing your product, it is easy to react defensively when the buyer asks something like: "What am I going to do with just another _____?" The buyer is not tearing down your "baby." Instead, the buyer is looking for ammunition to help him/her make a favorable decision. Who else but you should know why it is important to purchase your product? Remember that you are providing a solution (benefit) to the buyer.

Sales ability is acquired. We do it in all walks of life. Make the call once you are solidly prepared, and practice beforehand. Don't let your pitch sound canned. It does not take a lifetime to master the successful sales pitch.

Specialty food buyers appear to want the deal. They are not interested, ostensibly, in product quality, variety, choice, or "newness," per se. They want the product line that offers them the best deal—one with the most up-front profit.

The buyer/seller dialogues on the following page provide a small sampling of how you could respond to some of the more common objections.

*Examples of what **not** to say:*

Buyer: *"My color T.V. isn't working."*

You: *"I've had one sent to you from Macy's."*

Buyer: *"This stuff's too expensive!"*

You: *"Oh, here's $1,000 in cash to help you pay for it."*

GUIDELINES FOR SUCCESS
Handling Buyer Objections

Buyer: "I already have a dozen brands of mustard."

You: "Offering variety and choice is a specialty food trade strength. This is especially true in the mustard and condiment category."

Buyer: "Your competition offers a better deal."

You: "Let's compare the two deals, and I will consider meeting or 'bettering' it."

Buyer: "Your product is just too expensive."

You: "Ours offers the highest quality of any product in its category. It is more than worth the money. Why not let your customers decide?"

Buyer: "I have no more room in my product assortment."

You: "You can purchase a smaller beginning order—of the 'unique' item(s) in my line." (For example, if your line consists of five different condiments, offer the one that is really different, not readily available from other suppliers, as the lead.)

Buyer: "Not now." (This is very common.)
You: "If not now, then when?" Or, "What would it take to make the offer of interest now?" (There may not be much you can do about this, except to offer to come back, call, or make contact by mail later.)

Buyer: (a retailer) "I don't want to deal with another supplier."

You: "I can ship C.O.D., and save you the time and cost of setting up a new file/account."

Buyer: (a retailer) "I don't want to deal with another supplier."

You: "Can you give me the name of a distributor with whom you like dealing, and from whom you would consider buying my product?"

Buyer: (a distributor) "I don't want to do the pioneering your product requires in my territory."

You: (having made several successful sales calls in the distributor territory) "Here are a half dozen orders from retailers in your territory. All you have to do is deliver my product in your next shipment to them."

Buyer: (distributor who doubts worth of product) "We don't have any call for this product."

You: "People (retail customers) won't ask for products they know you don't have. Why not poll your retailer customers by phone or mail to determine the product's potential?"

Buyer: (who already buys similar products): "Why should I change suppliers and give you the business?"

You: "We're not asking you to abandon your current supplier—just let us supply you with a few items and let us prove our service and value to you."

Buyer: "Will you guarantee the product?"
You: "We will guarantee the product against defects and will replace or refund. We do not guarantee the sale of the product."

CHAPTER FOUR
PROCESSING ORDERS
AND OFFICE MANAGEMENT

Many new food producers devote too much of their time and energy to producing the product. They think about marketing the product only after it is produced. But, once the orders are in hand, what then? Order processing and office management are employed in preparing the paperwork associated with shipping and paying for the order.

Accounts Receivable Bookkeeping

It will be important for you to understand some basic accounting. It is called double entry accounting, and it is easy to learn. Perhaps the easiest is to retain the services of an accountant or bookkeeper; however many of you will not be able to afford this luxury in the early stages of your business development. Also, it will be necessary for you to understand the principles so you can communicate effectively with the bookkeeper.

Mr. Carl A. Lindblad, President of the Dedham (MA) financial systems company Rubicon, Inc., offers the following guidance: "From the very start, it is essential that you set up an accurate and informative bookkeeping system. An exhaustive study has revealed that of the eight primary causes of business failure six are financial. They are: insufficient capital, inventory mismanagement, overspending on fixed assets, too liberal a credit policy, taking too much out of the business, and too rapid growth. The other two are lack of experience, and wrong location. Furthermore, it should go without saying that your business should have a bank account separate from your personal account. Personal funds should not be co-mingled with business funds, and all transactions should go through the bank account and not through distant cash or other accounts.

"If you do not have a good working knowledge of bookkeeping, you should hire the services of a competent professional to set up your books and teach you how best to use them. This applies even if you are unable to afford a bookkeeper or ongoing services in the early stages of your business.

"In seeking professional help, check with friends and acquaintances to find a well-recommended accountant or bookkeeping professional. These may have designations all the way from CPA (Certified Public Accountant) to public accountant to a bookkeeping service.

"In your discussions with these firms, you will want to ascertain what sort of financial programs each offers. The more important systems include Income Statements, Balance Sheets, the General Ledger and Budget Statements. A brief description of each follows:

"The *Income Statement* is a historical report showing how your business did during a certain period. It is a primary source for business planning, and should contain such vital information as sales by product, cost by product, gross profit, expenses by type, and ratios used to monitor the financial health of the business.

"The *Balance Sheet* is a snapshot of the financial condition of the business at the time stated. It not only shows the net worth or 'book value' (assets minus liabilities) of your business, but also provides the remaining figures needed to calculate the important ratios of business analysis. Such ratios include liquidity, safety, profitability, and asset management. The ratios are important for financial control, and are used by bankers and other lenders when considering loans to the business. Your bookkeeping firm should be able to analyze the ratios of your business.

"The *General Ledger*, commonly called the 'books' of the company, records all of the day-to-day financial transactions. The more detail, for later understanding, the better. Supporting the General Ledger are subsidiary ledgers and records that may include: the Employee Ledger, Sales Journal, Purchase Journal, and Inventory Report.

"*Budget Statements* are estimates of future results. A carefully prepared budget will enable you to plan marketing strategy, production criteria, personnel needs, and financing requirement. A good budget not only supplies a reasoned road map for future operations but also yields essential information for potential lenders or investors. This is where you 'plan your work then work your plan.'

"The vital consideration in selecting a financial services professional is not the university degree or designation but the quality of training and the amount of experience such a person can bring to get your particular business headed in the right direction. Interview and compare the prices and experience of several such firms, and don't necessarily pick the cheapest one.

"Your system should include a complete set of books, monthly financial statements, required tax returns (which do require a professional) and an accurate and aged tracking of accounts receivable and accounts payable transactions. Anything less puts your business at risk.

"Essentially, accounts receivable bookkeeping is simply keeping track of who owes you money during a period in time. Usually, you will work on a monthly basis. I recommend that you employ a one-write system that reduces the chance of error, and saves time. With a one-write system, you use an Accounts Receivable Control Sheet and individual account ledger cards, along with a one-write binder. The control sheet allows you to keep track of sales and receivables during the month, and to allocate the funds involved using the columns provided.

"You make entries when transactions occur: sales (or debits) and receipts (or credits). Each account ledger card is filled alphabetically by customer name, which offers you an easy way of keeping track of each customer account. Much of the accounts receivable bookkeeping can be accomplished with the use of computer software programs."

Dunning

Dunning is what you do when the account you thought was going to pay on time doesn't. If your terms are NET 30 days, then around the 35th day, mail the first of three dunning letters/notes. See Appendix O for sample dunning letters.

About ten days after the final letter/telephone call, place the account into collection. There are a number of firms that provide this service. At the level of your activity, these firms will charge as much as forty percent of the invoice amount to make the collection. If they fail, they will recommend that you seek legal recourse (as a rule, this is only practical when used for amounts over $5,000.00). This can be very costly, usually more than either the invoice amount, or the amount that may be awarded in court. Consider writing the outstanding amount off as a bad debt (a factor that should be considered in your pricing under a "reserve for bad debts" category).

Tax Considerations

Depending on the style of company you establish (Proprietorship, Partnership, Corporation, Subchapter S Corporation), you may be required to file certain types of tax returns, both with the I.R.S. and with your state revenue service. The important thing to remember is to keep accurate and complete records of all your business income and expenditures. You will be well-advised to seek the advice of an accountant when you first set up your books. The process of meeting your tax obligations will be less cumbersome if you get the paperwork in order from the start.

Forms Usage and Filing

Many of your basic supplies including invoices, envelopes, price sheets, letterhead stationery, address labels, credit check forms, and dunning letter/forms can be designed with the help of a personal computer. Use a rubber stamp if you do not want to have 1,000 copies of something printed.

Invoices can be printed using carbonless paper. You will require four-part to six-part invoices. Some companies use only a two-part invoice, relying, instead, on photocopies and facsimiles to meet their requirements.

Naturally, you will want to maintain files of all your business correspondence, accounts receivable, accounts payable, completed sales transactions, etc. Generally, files are kept current for one year, then placed in a different drawer. Keep one current year file drawer, plus two others for the past two years. Files from earlier years may be retired to boxes and

The invoice parts are used for some or all of the following purposes:

Part 1. Customer
Part 2. Broker
Part 3. Accounts receivable
Part 4. Shipping confirmation
Part 5. Warehouse copy
Part 6. Packing slip

See Appendix O for sample forms.

GUIDELINES FOR SUCCESS
Order Processing Flow Chart

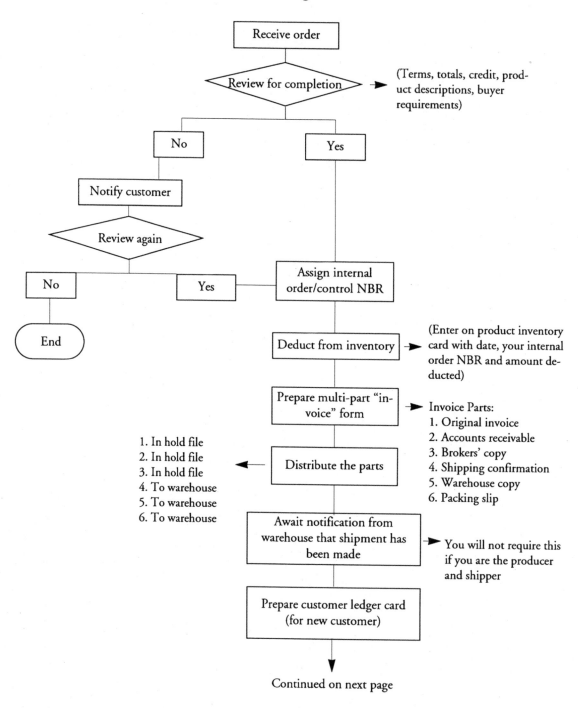

Continued on next page

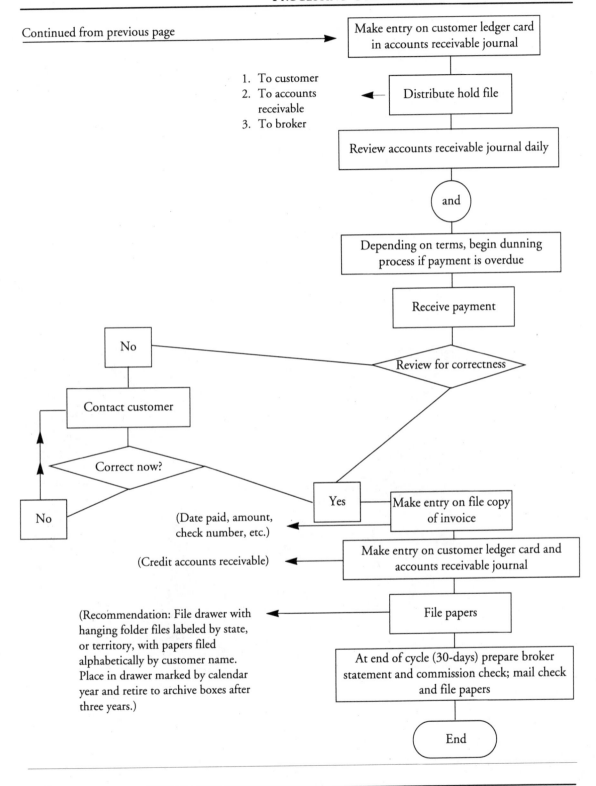

Continued from previous page

Make entry on customer ledger card in accounts receivable journal

1. To customer
2. To accounts receivable
3. To broker

Distribute hold file

Review accounts receivable journal daily

and

Depending on terms, begin dunning process if payment is overdue

Receive payment

Review for correctness

No

Contact customer

Correct now?

No

Yes

Make entry on file copy of invoice

(Date paid, amount, check number, etc.)

(Credit accounts receivable)

Make entry on customer ledger card and accounts receivable journal

(Recommendation: File drawer with hanging folder files labeled by state, or territory, with papers filed alphabetically by customer name. Place in drawer marked by calendar year and retire to archive boxes after three years.)

File papers

At end of cycle (30-days) prepare broker statement and commission check; mail check and file papers

End

should be stored for at least seven years (for tax purposes).

Filing should be set up in accordance with what makes life easier for you. Files should have some rationale that is easy to remember and easy to employ. A file set up for completed sales transactions alphabetically by geographic location is one of the easiest to use.

Order Processing Flow

Order processing supplies needed: A "one-write" accounting system, consisting of binder, journal forms, and ledger cards. Much of this can be accomplished with the aid of appropriate computer software[1]; however, the preceeding flow chart can be applied to understanding and clarifying both manual and computer applications.

[1]   One such piece of software is called "Maker's Automated Clerk," from Industrious Software Solutions, 504 North Oak St., Inglewood, CA 90302, (800) 351-4225.

DEVELOPING LONG-TERM CUSTOMER RELATIONSHIPS

The basic theory of good customer service is to operate for the convenience of your customer. This means that you call the customer back instead of asking the customer to return your call. You accept the responsibility for getting answers to customers' questions. Don't ask them to telephone someone else to get an answer. The examples are endless. Suffice it to say that many food producers fail to get the point about customer service: It is service to the customer.

One often overlooked aspect of marketing is the follow-up process after the order is shipped. Sometimes this is simply a telephone call, or visit, to see that all arrived in good order. This helps cement your professional relationship and it creates good-will. You impress the customer as someone who will stay around, and not run off with the check.

Consider telephone marketing, to insure that customer contact is maintained. In those areas where you are not using a broker, you can generate continued sales over the telephone. You can use the telephone and the mails to contact all your customers, regardless of broker use, regarding special promotions. Alert your broker of any subsequent interest so that a sales call can be made.

Customer Feedback Hint

Include a "customer satisfaction card" in your shipment or with your invoice to retailers. This can be a form that allows the customer to comment on the condition of the product or the nature of any of your services. It can also be designed as a convenient and easy-to-use re-order form.

CHAPTER FIVE
SUMMARY

We began this book by testing your motivation. You learned that obtaining nationwide distribution—in every grocery on every corner in every city and town—costs the market leaders a fortune. There are more than 10,000 new food products introduced every year, and there is a 96 percent failure rate over the first three years. Yet, here you are, now versed in the methods and procedures for marketing your specialty food product. Or, armed as you are with the knowledge, you have decided, or are about to decide, that it just is not for you. Perhaps, you are going to give it a good "think" before proceeding.

In either case, you are ahead of the game. You now know how to become a "focused niche player," and what is needed to get your product on the food store shelf.

CULTIVATING EFFECTIVE HABITS

Firefly

FIREFLY FOODS CO.
P.O. Box 82096, Portland, OR 97282

INGREDIENTS
cider vinegar, 5% acidity, red wine (contains sulfites),
basil, garlic

5 fl. oz.

Basil/Garlic Vinegar

If you have decided to go ahead, then take a lead from Stephen Covey's book, *The Seven Habits of Highly Effective People* (Simon and Schuster, New York, 1989), and incorporate these habits into your repetoire:

Habit 1: Be Proactive—Proactive people develop the ability to choose their response, making them more a product of their values and decisions than their moods and conditions.

Habit 2: Begin with the End in Mind—Effective people realize that things are created mentally before they are created physically. They write a mission or purpose statement and use it as a frame of reference for making future decisions. They clarify values and set priorities before selecting goals and going about the work.

Habit 3: Put First Things First—To "leverage" our time, we should devote less attention to activities that are urgent but unimportant, more time to those things that are important but not necessarily urgent. Use your business plan to help you keep on track.

Habit 4: Think Win-Win—Effective people model the win-win principle in their relationships and agreements. The win-win performance agreement clarifies expectations by making the following five elements very explicit: desired results, guidelines, resources, accountability, and consequences.

Habit 5: Seek First to Understand, Then to Be Understood—We see the world as we are, not as it is. Our perceptions come out of our experiences. Most credibility problems begin with perception differences. To resolve these differences and to restore credibility, one must exercise empathy, seeking first to understand the point of view of the other person. Remember to operate for the convenience of your customer.

Habit 6: Synergize—This is the habit of creative cooperation or teamwork. For those who have a win-win abundance mentality and exercise empathy, differences in any relationship can produce synergy, where the whole is greater than the sum of its parts.

Habit 7: *Sharpen the Saw*—The habit of sharpening the saw regularly means having a balanced, systematic program for self-renewal in the four areas of our lives: physical, mental, emotional-social, and spiritual.

Take these seven habits to heart. They will be useful in everything you do.

Throughout this book, I have tried to make sense of some of the more complex issues of specialty food cost accounting, market research, pricing, and distribution. The rest of it—production, packaging and labeling, for example—are all pretty matter of fact, save the visceral issues of what is or is not aesthetically appealing (taste, packaging, labeling, etc.).

Ultimately, you will have to just put your foot in the water. To paraphrase a famous saying, "Gourmet food marketing, like the frog, can be dissected, but in the process, the beast dies." Death by analysis. If you have that fire in your belly, and if you have the willpower, perseverance, motivation, focus, and self-discipline . . . and if you have the money, and the health, and the idea, the concept, the fever . . . then Do it and Good Profits To You!

I invite you to comment on this book, and/or to make any recommendations for future editions. If you are a service provider, please submit your company name and description of your service to be considered for listing in the next edition of *From Kitchen to Market*.

"Gourmet food marketing, like the frog, can be dissected, but in the process, the beast dies."

APPENDIX A
TRADE SHOWS

The following appendices are listings of services and sources of assistance and are meant to be neither conclusive nor to serve as an endorsement.

BOSTON GIFT SHOW

Boston, MA
Bayside Exposition Center
and World Trade Center
Contact: George Little Management, Inc.
212/686-6070

THE FINE FOODS SHOW

1099 Hingham St.
Rockland, MA 02370
Contact: Tara Burke
617/871-2700

THE GOURMET SHOW AT LOS ANGELES

Los Angeles Convention and Exhibition Center
Contact: George Little Management, Inc.
577 Airport Blvd. 4th Floor
Burlingame, CA 94010
Tel: 415/344-5171
FAX: 415/344-5270

INTERNATIONAL DAIRY-DELI-BAKERY SHOW

Contact: J. Treloar
202/296-4250

INTERNATIONAL GIFT BASKET, FLORAL AND BALLOON JUBILEE!

Contact: Festivities Publications, Inc.
1205 W. Forsyth St.
Jacksonville, FL 32204
904/634-1902

INTERNATIONAL FANCY FOOD AND CONFECTION SHOWS

Contact: NASFT
8 West 40th St.
New York, NY 10018
800/255-2502 or 212/505-1770

These are owned and sponsored by the National Association for the Specialty Food Trade, Inc. (NASFT), They are the largest association in the United States specializing in the representation and promotion of specialty food and confectionery products. It sponsors two very important semi-annual food shows for its members that attract buyers and decision-makers from all segments of the specialty food industry.

NATIONAL CANDY SHOW

King of Prussia, PA 19406
215/688-7207

NEW YORK GOURMET SHOW

The Accent on Housewares Showcase
Jacob Javits Center
New York, NY
Contact: George Little Management, Inc.
Susan G. Corwin, Show Manager
New York Food and Beverage Show
577 Airport Blvd. 4th Floor
Burlingame, CA 94010
Tel: 415/344-5171

The New York Gourmet Show is an annual show for gourmet food and beverage manufacturers and distributors. The attendee profile includes specialty and department store buyers, gift shops, importers and distributors, mail order/catalog houses, specialty food shops as well as restauranteurs, caterers and independent supermarket buyers.

S.I.A.L.

39, Rue de la Bienfaisance
75008, Paris, France
202/720-3425

Show held in October, even-numbered years.

ANUGA

World Food Market
Cologne, Germany
Contact: U.S.D.A., Room 4939
Washington, DC 20250-1000
Tel: 202/245-5182
FAX: 202/472-4374

Show held in October, odd-numbered years.

S.I.A.L. and ANUGA are biannual food shows that are particularly beneficial to European producers desiring to introduce products to the United States, and for U.S. producers wishing to export products to European markets.

FOOD PACIFIC

Canada's International Trade Show on Food
B.C. Place Stadium, Vancouver, B.C., Canada
Contact: Show Management, FOOD PACIFIC
190 - 10651 Shellbridge Limited
Richmond, B.C., Canada V6X 2W8
Tel: 604/276-2277

Food Pacific is an annual international food products and food processing equipment show. The largest segment of visitors at recent shows have been Canadian wholesaler/distributors.

The following international trade shows may be of some value to food producers ready to explore international markets. Contact the Foreign Agricultural Service, U.S.D.A., Room 4647, South Building, Washington, D.C. 20250-1000. Telephone: 202/245-5182/FAX: 202/472-4374

FOODEX JAPAN

International Food & Beverage Exhibition
Nippon Convention Center
U.S. Pavilion
Tokyo, Japan
Organized by Market Development International
Contact: Kam Vento 916/863-2518

HOFEX

International Hotel/Restaurant Food & Drink
Hong Kong
Organized by Hong Kong
Exhibition Services Ltd.

NASDA
NATIONAL ASSOCIATION OF STATE
DEPARTMENTS OF AGRICULTURE

1616 H Street, Washington, D.C. 20006
202/628-1566

This show is held in conjuction with the Food Marketing Institute's Supermarket Show.
Contact: Haidee Calore
703/876-0900

APPENDIX B
TRADE JOURNALS

The following list is neither conclusive nor is it mean to serve as an endorsement.

FANCY FOOD MAGAZINE

Talcott Communications Corp.
1529 Merchandise Mart
Chicago, IL 60654
312/670-0800

Primary focus: Specialty food.

FOOD ARTS

387 Park Avenue South
New York, NY 10016
212/684-4224

Primary focus: Restaurant food preparation, recipes, supplies.

FOOD DISTRIBUTION MAGAZINE

POB 10378-34617
912 Drew St., #64
Clearwater, FL 34615
813/443-2723

Primary focus: Specialty food. Managers of the
National Food Distribution Network (NFDN).

GIFT BASKET REVIEW

Festivities Publications, Inc.
1205 W. Forsyth St.
Jacksonville, FL 32204
904/634-1902

Primary focus: Gift trade.

GOURMET NEWS

United Publications, Inc.
POB 1056
Yarmouth, ME 04096
207/846-0600

Primary focus: A business newspaper for the
gourmet food trade. Publishers of the National
Directory of Gourmet Basket Retailers.

THE GOURMET RETAILER

3301 Ponce de Leon Blvd.
Suite 300
Coral Gables, FL 33134
305/446-3388
FAX: 305/446-2868

Primary focus: Specialty food/cookware.

THE GRIFFIN REPORT

GPC
1099 Hingham St.
Rockland, MA 02370
617/878-5300

Primary focus: Retail/chain/gourmet stores

NASFT SHOWCASE

8 West 40th St.
New York, NY 10018
212/505-1770

Primary focus: Specialty food.

PREPARED FOODS

Delta Communications, Inc.
455 N. Cityfront Plaza Drive
Chicago, IL 60611
312/222-2000

Primary focus: Grocery trade.

APPENDIX C
CO-PACKERS

The following is a partial listing of contract packaging companies (there are hundreds more). Using a contract packer will enable you to devote your time to management and marketing, while eliminating the enormous expense and responsibility of operating a production facility. Some will provide only the packaging, while others will help you with the entire formulation, production, packaging, and labeling process. Most offer no-cost initial consultation. Some even have marketing capability. This list is neither conclusive nor is it meant to serve as an endorsement.

AU PRINTEMPS GOURMET

C/O Fin D'Hiver Inc.
2875 Boulevard Labelle
Prevost,
Quebec, Canada J0R 1TO
Tel: 514/224-8221
FAX: 514/224-7943

Specific focus: herb and spice blends, whole fruits and liquors, jams and marmalades.

BERLIN PACKAGING

111 North Canal Street
Chicago, IL 60606
800/433-6417 or 312/876-9290

Specific focus: Berlin Packaging has fifteen
branch packaging locations throughout the U.S.

C.V. FINER FOODS

POB 88
Winthrop, ME 04364
Contact: Garth Vdoviak or Frank Carr III
Tel: 207/377-6221
FAX: 207/377-9655

Prefers manufacturers who already have formulas.

CALIFORNIA FOODS CORPORATION

P.O.Box 596
206 South Lilac Avenue
Rialto, CA 92376
Tel: 714/874-1500
FAX: 714/820-1863

CARTERET PACKAGING, INC.

1200 Milk Street
Carteret, NJ 07008
Tel: 908/969-1600
FAX: 908/969-9590

Specific focus: Specialty foods.

CHAUTAUQUA HILLS

Main St.
Sedan, KS 67361-5000
800/637-4101

Specific focus: Sauces and jams.

CHELTON HOUSE FOOD PRODUCTS

607 Heron Drive
P.O.Box 434
Bridgeport, NJ 08014
609/467-1600

CHRISTIE FOOD PRODUCTS, INC.

10 Charlam Dr.
Braintree, MA 02184
Tel: 617/848-7200
FAX: 617/848-7835

DIRIGO CORPORATION

141 West Second Street
South Boston, MA 02111
Tel: 800/345-9540
FAX: 617/268-9588

Specific focus: Can convert an at-home recipe into
a manufacturable formula. Has in-house lab for
additional product development and refinement.
Provides recipe protection.

DRAM PACKAGING, INC.

2 Central St.
Framingham, MA 01701
Tel: 508/788-0300
FAX: 508/847-6826
Specific focus: Mostly dry packaging. Welcomes short runs.

KIRKLAND CUSTOM CANNERY, INC.

640 8th Ave.
Kirkland, WA 98033
Tel: 206/828-4521
FAX: 206/889-9248

Specific focus: Cans, retort pouches, and fresh smoked packaging. Can do a run of less than 1000 (even just one dozen). Has nearby labeling connection.

LEMEE'S COMPANY

7 Alice Street
Conventry, RI 02816
401/821-2575

Specific focus: Hot packed specialty food co-packer. Short runs a specialty.

T. MARZETTI COMPANY

876 Yosemite Drive
Milpitas, CA 95035
Tel: 408/263-7540 or 800/888-3446
FAX: 408/263-0441

Specific focus: Mayonnaise, salad dressing, sauces, syrup. Mostly large runs.

Ontario Foods, Inc.

111-117 West Avenue
Albion, NY 14411
Tel: 716/589-4447
FAX: 716/589-6940

Specific focus: Mostly dry products, including
soups, drinks, noodles, sauces, rice.

Pisano Food Products, Inc.

261 King St.
Elk Grove Village, IL 60007
Tel: 708/640-7030
FAX: 708/640-6011

Specific focus: Cooks in several different ways.
Will produce, but will not sell, your product.
Helps with start-up formulations.

Ranney Ranch Company

301 North Harrison St. #287
Princeton, NJ 08540
Tel: 609-924-5133
FAX: 609/921-7293

Schlotterbeck and Foss

P.O.Box 8609
Portland, ME 04104
Tel: 207/772-4666
FAX: 207/774-3449

Specific focus: All kinds of private label, including
ice cream toppings, and salad dressings. Will help
with formulations and can provide full marketing
assistance.

STRATFORD MARK, LTD.

149 Grassy Plain St.
Bethel, CT 06801
203/748-7200

Specific focus: Salad dressings, relishes, sauces, and soups in glass containers. Can provide full guidance with label, package and legal procedures.

W. J. CLARK AND COMPANY

5400 West Roosevelt Road
Chicago, IL 60650
312/626-3676
FAX: 609/626-4064

THE WHIPPLE COMPANY

58 North Main Street
Natick, MA 01760
Tel: 508/653-2660
FAX: 508/653-2662

Specific focus: Full line of specialty foods.

VICTORIA PACKING CORPORATION

443 East 100th St.
Brooklyn, NY 11236
Tel: 718/927-3000
FAX: 718/649-7069

APPENDIX D
BROKER INFORMATION

NATIONAL ASSOCIATION OF SPECIALTY
FOOD AND CONFECTION BROKERS

P.O. Box 254
Tustin, CA 92680
714/838-5477

Request a copy of their 15-page directory, which
contains a specialty food broker profile.

APPENDIX E
DISTRIBUTOR INFORMATION

The following sources can be contacted for information regarding distributor listings. This list is neither conclusive nor is it meant to serve as an endorsement.

AMERICAN WHOLESALE MARKETERS ASSOCIATION
(Formerly National Candy Wholesalers Assn.)

1128 16th St. NW
Washington, D.C. 20036-4802
800/783-6292 or 202/463-2124

Send $36.00 for their member directory.

NASFT

8 West 40th Street
New York, NY 10018
212/505-1770 or 800/255-2502

NASFT will provide a member listing IF you are an NASFT member. For $15.00, they will provide you with a copy of the "Buyer's Guide" for the most recent International Fancy Food and Confection Show. The guide lists all of the exhibiting companies, but does not identify them by function (producer, broker, or distributor).

NATIONAL FOOD DISTRIBUTORS ASSOCIATION (NFDA)

111 East Wacker Drive
Chicago, IL 60601
312/644-6610

A member directory is available for members only. To join, request an application and send them the membership fee (minimum $250.00 for distributors, and $500.00 for producers—the amount depends on annual sales volume). In 1990, the NFDA made a concerted effort to report the findings of a study it commissioned that pointed to the increased use of specialty food distributors by retailers. It should be noted that the term "retailers," as used by the NFDA, means major retail organizations, not specialty food retailers.

THE NATIONAL FOOD DISTRIBUTION NETWORK (NFDN)

(GRO COM Group)
P.O. Box 10378
Clearwater, FL 34617
800/541-6336 or 813/443-2723

For an annual fee of $195.00, the NFDN will provide a one-year subscription to Food Distribution Magazine (FDM), as well as free listings in FDM directories. In addition, members receive broker, distributor, and buyer directories, plus a newsletter and a number of other services and savings.

THE THOMAS GROCERY REGISTER

460 Main Street
Wilmington, MA 01887
508/658-0440

Available from most public libraries.

The following is a very limited listing of specialty food distributors. This list is not conclusive nor is it meant to serve as an endorsement. Developing a distributor relationship is a function of product type, price, deal, and many other factors. The distributors listed here have strong specialty food orientations, and many are focusing increasing attention on grocery trade. This can result, generally, in "roll-out" difficulties for new products with small promotion budgets.

A.L. BAZZINI CO., INC.

339 Greenwich St.
New York, NY 10013
212/334-1280 or 800/228-0172

ANCO FOODS CORPORATION

149 New Dutch Lane
Fairfield, NJ 07004
201/575-9125

ATALANTA CORPORATION

Atalanta Plaza
Elizabeth, NJ 07206
908/351-8000

B & B SPECIALTY FOODS, INC.

4050 Stoneleigh Rd.
Bloomfield Hills, MI 48302
313/645-2096

BASCOM'S CORPORATION

495 River St.
Paterson, NJ 07524
201/345-1802

CHARLOTTE CHARLES, INC.

5990 West Touhy Ave.
Niles, IL 60648
708/647-0787

CHEX FINER FOODS

39 Franklin McKay Dr.
Attleboro, MA 02703
508/226-0660

COMMERCE FOODS, INC.

1133 Avenue of the Americas
Suite 3718
New York, NY 10036
212/398-0991

DORMAN-ROTH FOODS, INC.

14 Empire Blvd
Moonachie, NJ 07074
201/440-3600

EUROPA FOODS, LTD.

170 Commerce Drive
Hauppauge, NY 11788
516/273-0011

GERBAUD, INC.

217 East 85th Street, Suite 348
New York, NY 10028
212/628-2692

GOURMET AMERICA, INC.

350 Lincoln Street
Hingham, MA 02043
617/749-3140

HADDON HOUSE

250 Old Marlton Pike
P.O.Box 907
Medford, NJ 08055
609/654-7901

IMPORTS LIMITED

8001 East Fairmont Ave.
Scottsdale, AZ 85251
602/941-0557

INTERNATIONAL MARKETING SERVICES

501 5th Avenue
Suite 904
New York, NY 10017
212/697-1164

JARET INTERNATIONAL, INC.

2670 Stillwell Avenue
Brooklyn, NY 11224
718/946-1810

LIBERTY RICHTER, INC.

80 West Plaza One
Saddle Brook, NJ 07662
201/935-4500

MILLBROOK DISTRIBUTORS, INC.

P.O. Box 35
Route 56
Leicester, MA 01524
508/892-8171

NORTON NATIONAL MARKETERS GROUP

121 Kent Road
POB 162
Cornwall Bridge, CT 06754
203/672-0223

REESE FINER FOODS, INC.

300 Broadacres Drive
Bloomfield, NJ 07003
201/338-0300

WEATHERVANE FOODS

15 Linscott Road
Woburn, MA 01801
617/935-1000

APPENDIX F
FOODS BY MAIL

This list is neither conclusive nor is it meant to serve as an endorsement.

GOURMET DIGEST

2298 S. Elliot Rd., SW
Stockport, OH 43787-9741
614/557-3245
FAX: 614/557-3253

Gourmet Digest offers direct mail advertising in an "editorial-style" format. Good for the new-to-market specialty food producer.

WILLIAMS SONOMA

100 North Point Street
San Francisco, CA 94133
415/421-7900

Store Buyer: Sarah Esterling
Catalog Buyer: Tom O'Higgins

Appendix G
Catalog Preparation

These companies offer a complete package, from photography to printed sheets. You can order 2,000 to 2,500 catalog sheets with one color photograph, up to 50 words of typesetting copy, mechanical art, color separation, and full color printing on one side of an eighty-pound coated stock for prices that range from $425.00 to $485.00, depending upon which supplier you select. This list is neither conclusive nor is it meant to serve as an endorsement.

Catalog King

1 Entin Road
Clifton, NJ 07014
800/223-5751
201/472-1221

COLORLITH CORPORATION

777 Hartford Avenue
Johnston, RI 02919
800/556-7171
401/521-6000

COLOR TRACK, INC.

40 West 27th Street
New York, NY 10001
212/684-3660

CREATE-A-CARD, INC.

POB 85
Merrick, NY 11566
Tel: 800/753-6867
FAX: 516/420-5874

DIRECT PRESS/MODERN LITHO

386 Oakwood Road
Huntington Station, NY 11746
800/347-3285

DIRECT PRESS/MODERN LITHO

69 Dorman Ave.
San Francisco, CA 94124
800/735-7666

DYNAMIC COLOR CATALOGS

POB 1958
11 Richmond St.
Clifton, NJ 07011
800/466-1295 (In NJ: 201/772-8181)
FAX: 201/772-8924

KENNER PRINTING COMPANY

207 West 25th Street
New York, NY 10001
212/807-8800

MEGACOLOR CORPORATION

1380 S.W. 8th Street
Pompano Beach, FL 33069
800/367-2522
305/782-3600

PHOTOWORK

2946 San Pablo Avenue
Berkeley, CA 94702
510/548-0606

Appendix H
Government Sources

Code of Federal Regulations

The Code of Federal Regulations (CFR) contains the specific laws governing labels and ingredient statements for food products. Copies of the appropriate chapters may be purchased from your local government printing office.

State Departments of Commerce

Every state has a department of commerce and business development, usually located at the state capital. Its sole purpose is to promote and develop business within the state and offer new businesses information on state regulations and any legal requirements that apply. Many state departments of agriculture also have, or are related to, food marketing associations.

Food and Drug Administration

International Activities Branch
Center for Applied Nutrition FDA (HFS - 585)
200 C St., SW
Washington, DC 20204

Request free copy of information on how to start a food business.

APPENDIX I
MARKETING AND
FOOD MARKET RESEARCH

This list is neither conclusive nor is it meant to serve as an endorsement.

CONNECTICUT SPECIALTY FOOD AND BEVERAGE ASSOCIATION

262 Cedar Ridge Drive
Glastonbury, CT 06033
203/633-3826

This association has published a directory of resources essential to food producers. The book includes listings of glass manufacturers, box manufacturers, basket companies, packaging and bag businesses, printers, label designers, co-packers, truckers, food technologists, public relations agencies, etc.

THE FOOD INSTITUTE

American Institute of Food Distribution, Inc.
28-12 Broadway
Fair Lawn, NJ 07410
Tel: 201/791-5570
Contact: Mr. Roy Harrison, President

The Food Institute is a non-profit information clearinghouse maintained by dues from approximately 2,800 member companies throughout the food industry. It disseminates information to its members via a weekly report: *The Food Institute Report.*

FOOD MARKETING INSTITUTE

1750 K Street NW
Washington, D.C. 20006
202/452-8444

The Food Marketing Institute is a non-profit association conducting programs in research, education and public affairs on behalf of its 1,600 members, composed largely of multi-store chains, small regional firms and independent supermarkets.

FOOD MARKETING INTERNATIONAL

25 Church Street
Dedham, MA 02026
Tel: 617/326-3443
FAX: 617/326-3475

Founded in 1981 as a division of S. Richard Hall & Company, Inc., Food Marketing International is involved in specialty foods distribution, marketing, market research, and business development. On a fee basis, the firm prepares Specialty Food Marketing Action Plans that include specific and quantifiable milestones and budgets for new-to-market specialty food producers and importers/distributors.

THE GROCERY MANUFACTURERS OF AMERICA INC. (G.M.A.)

1010 Wisconsin Avenue, N.W.
Suite 800 Washington D.C. 20007
202/337-9400

G.M.A. is a trade association of the manufacturers and processors of food and non-food products sold primarily in retail grocery stores in the U.S. Readers may wish to request a copy of their 1990 publication: "Managing the Process of Introducing and Deleting Products in the Grocery and Drug Industry." The cost is $10.00.

THE GROWER'S GREEN BOOK

New World Publishing
3701 Clair Drive
Carmichael, CA 95608
916/944-7932

The Grower's Green Book, by Eric Gibson, is a guide to profitable produce marketing that covers marketing plans, research, crop selection, and selling through farmers markets, restaurants, roadside markets, pick-your-own operations and retail outlets. It is a comprehensive how-to book of high value produce marketing.

APPENDIX J
PACKAGING DESIGN

These companies supply and design packages. This list is neither conclusive nor is it meant to serve as an endorsement.

KREPE-KRAFT, INC.

4199 Bay View Rd.
Blasdell, NY 14219
Tel: 716/826-7086
FAX: 716/826-7239

PACKAGEMASTERS, INC.

P.O.Box 1183
52 Sindle Avenue
Little Falls, NJ 07424
Tel: 201/890-7511
FAX: 201/890-0470

SPECIALTY FOOD PACKAGING DESIGN

PBC International
One School St.
Glen Cove, NY 11542
516/676-2727

This book, written by New York Public Library
Culinary Collection head, Reynaldo Alejandro, in
association with the NASFT, contains more than
200 examples of specialty food package design.
The book may be purchased from PBC for
$60.00 per copy. NASFT member discount is
30%.

Appendix K
Packaging Materials

T hese companies are known to provide specialty food containers and packaging materials. There are hundreds of others, and you should check available listings for some near you. This list is not meant to serve as an endorsement.

AB Specialty Packaging, Inc.

Hialeah, FL 33014
Tel: 305/821-5901
FAX: 305/557-4975
and Fowler, IN 47944
Tel: 317/884-1040
FAX: 317/884-1317

AKM Packaging, Inc.

43 Clematis Rd.
Agawam, MA 01001
800/836-6256
FAX: 413/786-8097

CALPACK CONTAINER COMPANY

14518 Best Avenue
Santa Fe Springs, CA 90670
Tel: 310/802-7769 or 800/525-2109
FAX: 310/802-0817

Other locations in California, Oregon, and
Arizona.

DRISCOLL LABEL CO., INC.

1275 Bloomfield Ave.
Fairfield, NJ 07004
Tel: 201/575-8492
FAX: 201/575-8345

LABELS PLUS

2407 106th St. SW
Everett, WA 98204
Tel: 206/745-4592 or 800/275-7587
FAX: 206/523-1973

POLYFOAM PACKERS

2320 South Foster Avenue
Wheeling, IL 60090
Tel: 800/323-7442
FAX: 708/398-0653

ROBBINS CONTAINER CORPORATION

222 Conover St.
Brooklyn, NY 11231
Tel: 718/875-3204
FAX: 718/797-3529

APPENDIX L
BUSINESS LISTS

T his list is neither conclusive nor is it meant to serve as an endorsement.

AMERICAN BUSINESS INFORMATION, INC.

POB 27347
Omaha, NE 68127
402/331-7169

Business listings compiled from nationwide Yellow Pages.

COMPILERSPLUS, INC.

466 Main St.
New Rochelle, NY 10801
800/431-2914
(in New York State: 914/633-5240)

All listings (from Yellow Pages) are verified by telephone.

APPENDIX M
UNIFORM PRODUCT CODE

UNIFORM PRODUCT CODE:
UNIFORM CODE COUNCIL, INC.

8163 Old Yankee Rd.
Suite J
Dayton, OH 45458
513/435-3870
Contact: Mr. Harold P. Juckett, Executive
Vice President

The Uniform Code Council is the central management and information center for manufacturers and retailers participating in the system.
Current cost of registration is $300.00.

APPENDIX N
WOMEN IN THE FOOD INDUSTRY

This list is neither conclusive nor is it meant to serve as an endorsement.

NATIONAL ASSOCIATION FOR FEMALE EXECUTIVES

127 West 24th St.
New York, NY 10011
212/645-0770

Publishers of *Executive Female* magazine.

NATIONAL ASSOCIATION OF WOMEN BUSINESS OWNERS

221 N. LaSalle St.
Suite 2026
Chicago, IL 60601
312/346-2330

OFFICE OF WOMEN'S
BUSINESS OWNERSHIP
U.S. SMALL BUSINESS ADMINISTRATION

1441 L St. NW,
Rm 414
Washington, DC 20416
Tel: 202/653-8000

ROUNDTABLE FOR WOMEN
IN FOODSERVICE INC.

425 Central Park West,
Suite 2A
New York, NY 10025
Tel: 212/865-8100
FAX: 212/688-6457

APPENDIX O
SAMPLE FORMS

CREDIT APPLICATION

PRICE LIST/ORDER FORM

INVOICE

BROKER COMMISSION STATEMENT

STATEMENT OF ACCOUNT

DUNNING LETTERS

SAMPLE APPLICATION FOR CREDIT

Application For Credit

Date: _____

Company Name: _____
Business Address: _____

_____

Mailing Address: _____

City, State, Zip: _____

Phones: _____

Type of business: _____

Year business started: _____ Years at present location: _____

Type   ☐ Private Corporation   ☐ Partnership

       ☐ Public Corporation   ☐ Individual

Officers — Name	Position	Home Address	Phone

Banking References

1st Bank: _____

2nd Bank: _____

Trade References

1st Firm: _____

2nd Firm: _____

3rd Firm: _____

Credit Limit Requested: $ _____

In making this application for credit, the customer agrees to pay all invoices within 30 days from date of invoice and to pay a service charge of 1-1/2% per month, which is an annual percentage rate of 18% on all overdue balances. In the event a suit is necessary to collect any amount, the customer agrees to pay the seller's reasonable attorney fees and costs including attorneys fees for appeal.

Signature: _____ Title: _____ Date: _____

SAMPLE PRICE LIST

Product or Company Name

Sales Message/Testimonial

Retailer Price List and Order Form   Date:

Cases Ordered	Description	Case Pack	Case Lbs. Shipping Wt.	Unit Price	Case Price
_____	New Gourmet Condiment	12/8 Oz. Jar	9	$ 3.75	$ 45.00
_____	New Gourmet Condiment	12/12 Oz. Jar	14	7.00	84.00

Bill To:_____   Ship To:_____

Address:_____   Address:_____

City: _____ State:___ Zip:_____   City: _____ State:___ Zip:_____

Special Handling Instructions:_____

Customer Order Number: _____   Your Company Number: _____

Terms: C.O.D. Until Credit Approved, then Net 30 days, F.O.B. my warehouse
　　　 Prices subject to change without notice.

Thank You For Your Order

If available, this space should be used for more product and promotional data

My Company Name, Address, Telephone, Fax, Etc.

SAMPLE INVOICE

Your Company Name
Address
City, State, Zip
Telephone:
Fax:

Date:
No. :
Your Order No. :

Sold To:
*
*
*

Shipped To:
*
*
*

Our No.	Salesperson	Terms	F.O.B.	Ship Date	Shipped Via

Ordered	Shipped	Description	Unit Price	Amount

–THANK YOU FOR YOUR ORDER–
(prices subject to change without notice)

FREIGHT

TOTAL DUE $

SAMPLE BROKER STATEMENT

Your Company Name
Broker Commission Statement

Broker Name: _____ Period From: _____ To: _____

	Date	Order	Account	Invoice Amount	Rate	Amount
1						
2						
3						
4						
5						
6						
7						
8						
9						
10						

TOTAL >>>

Comments: _____

Total Commission: [   ]
Less Advance/Credit: [   ]
Commission Payable: [   ]

SAMPLE STATEMENT

STATEMENT

To:

Number:	
Statement Date:	
Terms:	
Customer No.:	

Item	Date	Description	Charge	Credit	Balance
Previous Balance Brought Forward >>>					

Thank You For Your Business   Please pay this amount   >>>

SAMPLE DUNNING LETTER (AT THE 33rd DAY)

Your Company Name
Address
Telephone Number

Date:
To:
Reference: Invoice number _____ of _____ (date)
Subject: Friendly reminder

To whom it may concern:

Our records indicate that the above referenced invoice remains unpaid.
Please comply with our terms and remit $ _____ to us immediately.

Let us know if your records do not concur with ours, and thank you for
your attention.

Sincerely,

SAMPLE DUNNING LETTER (AT THE 45th DAY)

Your Company Name
Address
Telephone Number

Date:
To:
Reference: Invoice number _____ of _____ (date)
Subject: Second notice

To whom it may concern:

We still show an amount due of $ _____ for the referenced invoice.
Please contact us immediately if you feel there has been an error.
Otherwise we expect your remittance now.

Sincerely,

SAMPLE DUNNING LETTER (AT THE 60th DAY)

Your Company Name
Address
Telephone Number

Date:
To:
Reference: Invoice number _____ of _____ (date)
Subject: Final Notice

To whom it may concern:

We have yet to receive payment of the referenced invoice. Since the amount due is now 60 days late, and in violation of our terms, we have no other recourse except to place your account into collection which we would rather not do. To avoid this upleasant action, please remit $ _____ now!

Sincerely,

APPENDIX P
SAMPLE BROKER
APPOINTMENT LETTER

(This is a very formal version—you may use a simpler form to suit your needs.)

AGREEMENT between [your company], a [corporation, proprietorship, partnership, as appropriate] ("Company"), whose principal office is located at [your address], and [broker name], a [corporation, etc., as appropriate] of [state] with principal office located at [address].

In consideration of the mutual covenants contained herein, the parties agree as follows:

Article I

APPOINTMENT

Company hereby appoints [broker name] its exclusive representative for sales of all the Company's [indicate product types, if necessary] throughout the Territory, as designated below, on the following terms and conditions.

Article II

TERRITORY

Territory means the [insert territory]. [Indicate any variations, accounts not included, etc.]

Article III

AUTHORITY

[Broker name] shall promote the sale of the Company's products according to its best judgement, including carrying out the following activities:

A. Establishing and supervising all field sales;

B. Contracting and servicing dealers, suppliers, retailers, wholesalers, and other users and purchasers for resale;

C. Assessing marketing strengths and weaknesses (prices, competition, and other contractual terms);

D. Recommending and implementing, if requested, advertising and promotional strategies and activities;

E. Receiving and transmitting orders and other requests from customers.

Article IV

RIGHT TO SOLICIT AND ACCEPT ORDERS

[Broker name]'s authority includes the exclusive right to solicit and accept orders, either directly or through it sales agents in the territory, for all products of the Company. Company agrees to transmit regularly to [broker name] all information concerning orders and sales that the Company receives or obtains directly, whether from existing customers or from third parties. [Broker name] will supply the Company its best field information on credibility for any new account and will maintain field surveillance on established accounts in terms of stability/ credibility. Company has the responsibility and authority to control credit line and terms to the customer.

Article V

COMMISSION ON SALES

Unless specified otherwise:

A. [Broker name] shall be entitled on all orders shipped by the Company to a commission of 10%

for sales to retailers, and 5% for sales to distributors.

B. The commission will be calculated on the total dollar amount of the order F.O.B. [your warehouse location].

Article VI

DEVOTION OF TIME AND SKILL

A. [Broker name] agrees to use its best efforts to promote the sales and use of, and to solicit and secure orders for, the products of the Company within the Territory.

B. [Broker name] shall observe Company policies, as provided in writing by the Company, as regards the sales of Company's products and shall be furnished regularly with sales literature, technical data and sample products by the Company, in reasonable quantities and without charge.

C. [Broker name] shall not participate in the sale of any product that would conflict with the products of the Company included in this agreement without the authorization of the Company.

Article VII

EXPENSES

Except as herein provided, [broker name] agrees to assume all expenses of its own employees, and all expenses of maintaining its organization as the sales representatives of the Company's products within the Territory and all expenses of sales agents or brokers retained by [broker name]. [Broker name] will identify and recommend advertising and promotional opportunities which, if agreed to by the Company, will be paid for by the Company.

Article VIII

COMPANIES REPRESENTED

[Broker name] will provide to the Company a list of all companies that it represents.

Article IX

DURATION OF AGREEMENT: TERMINATION

This agreement shall be effective from the execution hereof, and shall be binding on the parties hereto and their assigns, representatives, heirs, and successors. This agreement shall continue in effect for one year, and be automatically renewable annually thereafter until terminated by either party on thirty (30) days written notice to the other, provided, that in the event of insolvency or adjudication in bankruptcy or on the filing of a petition therefor by either party, this agreement may be terminated immediately at the option of either party on written notice to the other. Termination shall be without prejudice to the rights and obligations of the parties hereto that have vested prior to the effective date of termination, except that, on termination, the Company shall pay [broker name] the commissions provided only on orders received by the Company prior to the effective date of such termination and delivered to customers within ninety (90) days following the effective date of such termination. The acceptance, however, of such orders and the liability of the Company for the payment of commissions thereon are to be subject to the terms and conditions herein before provided.

Article X

CHANGES; ALTERATIONS

No change, alteration, modification or amendment to this agreement shall be effective unless in writing and properly executed by the parties hereto.

Article XI

APPLICABLE LAW

This agreement and any disputes relating thereto shall be construed under the laws of [your state], United States of America.

Article XII

CONTRACT TERMS EXCLUSIVE

This agreement constitutes the entire agreement between the parties hereto and the parties acknowledge and agree that neither of them has made any representation with respect to the subject matter of this agreement or any representations inducing the execution and delivery hereof except as specifically set forth herein and each of the parties hereto acknowledges that it has relied on its own judgment in entering into the same.

IN WITNESS WHEREOF, the parties have executed this agreement:

This _____ day of _____, 19_____

By: _____   By:_____
    (your company name)   (broker name)

_____   _____
   title   title

Appendix Q
Specialty Food
Market Profiles

As part of your market research, you will find it useful to know something about current product category trends in the specialty food industry. More comprehensive information is contained in studies available from Frost & Sullivan, Inc., and from Packaged Facts, both located in New York, as well as other sources.

I have provided a brief profile of some of the major product categories that includes discussion of product type, positioning, and circumstances that have impacted recent consumption trends.

BEVERAGES

Specialty beverages include coffee and tea, bottled sparkling water, natural sodas, flavored seltzer, certain soft drinks, and juices.

The specialty beverage leader is coffee and tea. In fact, coffee is the number one specialty product category. Overall consumption of coffee has decreased over the past decade, but consumption of specialty coffees has increased. Much of the demand is for coffee beans that can provide a fresher cup than vacuumed-packed ground coffee. Decaffeinated coffee is in demand as well, along with flavored coffees.

Most specialty coffees are promoted on the strength of their freshness and taste. Many are offered as special blends, among which Irish Cream, Chocolate, Amaretto and Hazelnut are best sellers.

Specialty tea includes both tea products and a variety of other non-camellia sinensis (tea) forms, including tonics, infusions, barks, and the like. As with coffee, overall consumption of tea is down, but consumption of specialty teas is up.

Specialty tea is sold in both loose and tea bag varieties. It is positioned in all kinds of retail outlets, and has shown a marked sales increase in fancy restaurants and hotels.

An example of a successful specialty tea transitioning from the specialty market to exclusively supermarket is Celestial Seasonings. This product can no longer be considered a specialty food product. Another tea line, Twinings, appears to successfully straddle the line between grocery and specialty distribution, depending on the varietal blend. For example, Twining's English Breakfast and Earl Grey teas are most likely to be seen in supermarkets, while its Lapsang Souchong and Russian Caravan varieties remain solidly placed in the specialty market.

The market for bottled sparkling water has many variants in the specialty food industry. Most major brands are now distributed outside of specialty food channels. These brands include San Peligreno, Poland Spring, Perrier, Evian, etc.

Who knew that we would become so concerned with our tap water that we would spend billions of dollars on bottled versions that, by regulation, have to meet standards no more rigorous than those for tap water?

Sodas, seltzer, soft drinks, non-alcoholic spritzers, and certain juices comprise the remainder of this category.

CHEESE AND DAIRY PRODUCTS

In the 1980's, the specialty cheese sector was one of the fastest growing in the gourmet food market. Increased consumer awareness of so-called "healthy" foods influenced a decline in sales of the high-fat varieties. Brie remains in strongest demand, followed by aged cheddar, fresh curd cheese, soft ripened cheese, Swiss cheese, and blue mold cheese.

Some specialty food stores carry several hundred cheese varieties; hence, with this kind of variety, most consumers have yet to develop a brand preference.

To further busy this market, producers have introduced "light-style" cheese and even newer varieties, such as chevre (goat) cheese. European-style cheese has been introduced by U.S. producers, and by U.S. manufacturing subsidiaries of overseas cheese companies. It is in this latter area that the greatest opportunity for specialty cheese growth exists.

Another specialty food product in this category is superpremium ice cream and frozen yogurt. The former came charging into the market in the 1970's, lead by Häagen Dazs. By our definition, this can no longer be considered a specialty food. Despite the huge fat content, superpremium ice cream is an example of an affordable luxury— some go so far to tout its medicinal value (eases emotional stress, etc.)—and there are numerous regional superpremium ice creams on the market. Notable is the Ben & Jerry's brand. Many are hand packed and offer the consumer exotic flavors such as Praline Caramel Swirl and Mint Chocolate.

Watch for this category to be picked up increasingly by the major ice cream producers as they attempt to clone the flavor and fat content offered by the smaller producers.

The other notable part of this category is frozen yogurt, especially soft served. Growth in frozen yogurt consumption now exceeds that of super-premium ice cream, especially the low-fat and fat free varieties. Even Häagen Dazs now offers a branded frozen yogurt. Still, most frozen yogurt is made and sold in the same place, making it an improbable product for you to consider selling in retail packages.

There being only so much room in the nation's freezer cases, it is unlikely that you will be able to garner a niche without a sizeable investment. The frozen food segment, in total, is considered to be the hardest to penetrate in the food industry. This is no less the case with superpremium ice cream and frozen yogurt.

CRACKERS AND BREADS

Crackers are more important to consumers than cookies, according to a U.S. Department of Commerce report. In its Annual Household Penetration of Selected Grocery Items, the Department noted that crackers held more than 98% versus 95% for cookies. Even so, cookies account for more than 50% of the total snack foods market.

In the specialty food industry, crackers are used to serve other products, such as cheese and dips. Yet, crackers in grocery stores tend to be positioned as a food product in and of itself with its own characteristic flavor.

The big sellers tend to be high in fiber and low in salt. They appeal to a broad consumer interest in health and fitness. An even newer product type is the fat free or low-fat cracker. Nearly every specialty food store carries a variety of specialty crackers.

Your chance to make a dent will be based on your ability to produce a unique cracker. It appears that the major food companies have been eager to copy successful specialty crackers under their own brands. Examples include Keebler's "Stone Creek," Nabisco's "American Classic" line, and Pepperidge Farms' (a Campbell Soup subsidiary) "Distinctive Crackers" line. The cracker segment is a big one, with a wide assortment, and consumers always seem interested in trying new varieties.

Breads, on the other hand, are positioned differently than crackers. Breads include the bake-off variety that are offered fresh by the retailer. This segment includes French and Italian breads, rolls, bagels and other types. They also include crispbreads and Lavosh that are baked, packaged and shipped in retail containers.

A related product is potato chips, especially those that are prepared with low sodium and fat content. Also growing in popularity are tortilla chips made from various types of corn.

CONDIMENTS

The specialty condiments' segment of the specialty market constitutes hundreds of products. Among them are mustard, sauce, catsup, relish, pepper, olives, chutney, oil, horseradish, mayonnaise, vinegar, herbs and spices, and seasoning.

Most are positioned as high quality, exotic, uniquely flavored products compared to the grocery trade variants. The specialty condiment category has produced many of the products that have become mainstream grocery products. An example is Grey Poupon Dijon mustard. Distribution of this white wine flavored variant began in the specialty food industry. It is now available in every supermarket and in almost all restaurants.

The dominant condiment is mustard. With more than five dozen brands on the market at any time, each manufacturer attempts to provide the ever experimenting consumer with yet another taste sensation. Those that survive do so with a true sense of focused niche marketing.

Other specialty condiments include chutney, extra virgin olive oils, flavored vinegars, avocado oils, spice pastes, flavored mayonnaise, salad dressings, and a variety of Tex-Mex, Caribbean, Thai and stir-fry sauces.

Specialty herbs, spices and seasonings form an important and growing part of the specialty condiment segment. Many are offered as fresh packaged herb blends, or as dips and mixes that can be blended easily with mayonnaise, yogurt and/or sour cream to make a tasty and interesting hors d'oeuvre or appetizer.

Specialty condiments are positioned in a variety of packages, including glass jars, plastic and aseptic containers, and tubes. Only shelf-stable salad dressings stick to the traditional long-necked salad dressing jar.

SPECIALTY MEAT AND SEAFOOD

Ranch buffalo, pâté de foie gras, country pâtés, terrines, unusual sausage, boar, venison, fowl, escargot, and certain deli meats are included in the specialty meat category. Seafood includes smoked salmon, caviar, eel, and certain fish.

Sales of these products are driven by consumers characterized by ethnic demographics. Their interest is in taking foods they remember from their experience in another country, or from association with particular ethnic habits and traditions.

Specialty fish consumption is on the increase, primarily due to consumer interest in its lower fat and cholesterol content. As a result, there has been an increase in aquaculture devoted to farming and marketing specialty fish, especially smoked salmon and smoked trout, and catfish.

CONFECTION

The category includes chocolate, cakes, cookies, and candy. This is where the term "sinfully delicious" has the most meaning. Specialty confections appeal to a broad audience comprising people of all backgrounds and ages. Their allure is nearly universal—truly, the affordable luxury.

About this industry, the saying goes, tongue in cheek: "What I need is another chocolate and another mustard line." Talk about widely over assorted! In any case, chocolate reigns with new varieties introduced every day. The most recent is a 5" x 7" Chocolate Macadamia Monet "painting," in which a painting by Claude Monet is brushed on a chocolate base with special confectioner's paint. Another example is a solid chocolate cellular phone!

Chocolate is now sold both in chocolate boutiques (Godiva, as an example), and in fancy retail packages. We pay upwards of $25.00 a pound for this indulgence. Very few chocolates have been successfully branded in the specialty food industry. Most that have succeeded did so with strong capital backing by large overseas chocolate companies, such as Tobler, Lindt, and Cadbury.

Many American chocolate companies have introduced high quality products. What distinguishes most of them from the rest is the inclusion of cocoa butter that provides high quality chocolate with a distinctive aroma and smoothness. This, plus interesting retail packaging and extensive promotion, helps carve out a profitable niche.

Specialty cookies are noted for their high quality content and imaginative ingredients. Among these are delicious tasting pistachio rum, double chocolate macadamia nut, and a variety of fancy chocolate chip cookies.

Other varieties include high quality low-fat, and no fat, cookies, and biscuits imported from Italy (panetonne), France, and Great Britain (shortbread).

Fancy cakes, those with extremely rich tasting ingredients (mostly chocolate) and with generous infusions of alcohol flavorings, have made a dent in the industry. Most are positioned for the hotel and restaurant trade, but many are sold via fancy retail outlets. They tend to be special occasion cakes, with strong seasonal sales. Many supermarkets have upgraded their baking products by offering made-to-order fancy cakes. Among the most popular appear to be carrot cake and fancy chocolate cake.

Specialty candies make up the remainder of the category and the best examples are imported hard candies from Europe and Japan. Most make their inroad by offering flavors not ordinarily associated with candy, such as kiwi, and mango fruit. Others have caught consumer interest by being favored by famous people (personality endorsements), such as "gourmet" jelly beans. Even though few of these meet our definition of a specialty product, many have been introduced successfully through the specialty food trade.

JAMS, JELLIES AND PRESERVES

A vast assortment of jams, jellies and preserves have been made available to the consumer by major food processors. An even wider assortment is available from cottage industries. It is from the latter that many of the new specialty food products have grown.

In both cases, the highest quality products are those that have little or no added sugar (some are sweetened only with apple or grape juice), no pectin, no artificial colors or flavors, and no preservatives. The imported jams and preserves with highest quality are those where the ingredients indicate more fruit than sugar. Many of these fancy jams are expensive and require refrigeration after opening.

Almost the entire market consists of retail packaged product. A small percentage is made available in bulk sizes for institutional and food service use, with some packaged in small containers for restaurant, table top use.

Success, in terms of developing large volume, will be limited to the major producers, or, as in the case of Polaner All Fruit jams, to those producers who offer a new product at the right price not available from the major companies. It is much too easy to clone a jelly or jam recipe to suggest that yours will take over shelf space from Kraft or Welch's, for example.

FOOD TO GO

Prepared foods are offered by many, if not, all specialty food retail stores. They are of the type and quality one would expect from a consumer demanding both high quality ingredients and good taste.

This is among the fastest growing segment of the specialty food industry. It is especially popular with the "DINKS" population segment (double income, no kids) because it offers quick and easy solutions to dinner preparation. The food is high quality fast food far removed from delivered pizza. One can purchase, all at once, a cold fruit soup, a freshly baked smoked-ham-and-brie tart, or an asparagus lasagna, and a rich, calorie-laden dessert. Most foods to go are sold from a refrigerated case, and very few are branded.

What you need to know about prepared specialty foods will help only if you are planning to open a retail outlet, or sell a locally prepared refrigerated product to retailers in your region. By the time you go beyond that area, the product falls into another category—a retail packaged food that will require some preparation before it can be consumed.

MISCELLANEOUS SPECIALTY FOODS

This category involves the remainder of specialty food items. It includes, among others, pasta, mushrooms, rice, snackfoods, baked goods, soups, honey, truffles, vegetables, legumes, fruits, and rice.

One of the leaders is pasta, which follows understandably from the growing consumption of the category. Average annual consumption now exceeds 17 pounds per capita.

Mushroom consumption has increased also, especially for fresh mushrooms. More than three quarters of all mushrooms are sold fresh, just the opposite of what pertained 20 years ago when most mushrooms were sold processed. The specialty mushrooms, which include shitake, morel, Italian Brown, and chanterelle are sold in both fresh and processed versions. They appeal to a small audience, largely composed of chefs and institutional food service accounts.

Wild rice, especially Basmati and American wild, and are available in dry packages and as rice mixes. Most of the growth for American rice is abroad.

Snackfoods abound, and most in the specialty industry consist of high quality dried fruits, nuts, "trail mixes," and certain crackers. Successful specialty snackfoods are those that have the right combination of high quality and low price in order to appeal to a wide audience.

Specialty soups are available in numerous varieties. Notable among them are the Knorr's, Mayacamma, Pepperidge Farm, and Baxters (from Scotland). Most of these tend not to duplicate available flavors. Royal Game, Pheasant, Lobster Bisque, Mulagatawny, Senegalese, and vegetable korma are some of the fancy soups now on the market.

The proliferation of dried soup mixes versus canned condensed or ready to serve soups is apparent. Producing these requires less capital, and shipping and storing the product is less expensive for the new specialty food marketer.

Produce has always played a part in the specialty food market. Fruits, such as the kiwi and mango, and vegetables, such as salad greens and the already mentioned mushrooms, continue to offer up interesting variations for the consumer. Your only interest in this category probably will be for personal consumption, unless you want to use an interesting vegetable or dried fruit in a specialty retail packaged concoction.

Much of the growth of miscellaneous specialty foods will come from expanding consumer interest generated from exposure to "designer" menus in upscale, health and nutrition-oriented, restaurants.

SUMMARY

Success in the specialty food industry can be achieved by those entrepreneurs willing to adopt the specialty food perspective. Such a perspective requires a willingness to accept a floating bottom line, as well as strong perseverance and a skilled promotional savvy.

As you may have discerned from this mini-profile of the industry, there are many opportunities for a focused niche approach, where competition abounds, and a few opportunities for the producers who have products everyone demands, where sales growth can be phenomenal.

Regardless of your approach, a knowledge of industry trends, competition, stimulants and constraints to product growth will be invaluable to the new product marketer.

INDEX